THE INVISIBLE CITY

The Invisible City explores urban spaces from the perspective of a traveller, writer, and creator of theatre to illuminate how cities offer travellers and residents theatrical visions while also remaining mostly invisible, beyond the limits of attention.

The book explores the city as both stage and content in three parts. Firstly, it follows in pattern Italo Calvino's novel *Invisible Cities*, wherein Marco Polo describes cities to the Mongol emperor Kublai Khan, to produce a constellation of vignettes recalling individual cities through travel writing and engagement with artworks. Secondly, Gillette traces the Teatro Potlach group and its ongoing immersive, site-specific performance project Invisible Cities, which has staged performances in dozens of cities across Europe and the Americas. The final part of the book offers useful exercises for artists and travellers interested in researching their own invisible cities.

Written for practitioners, travellers, students, and thinkers interested in the city as site and source of performance, *The Invisible City* mixes travelogue with criticism and cleverly combines philosophical meditations with theatrical pedagogy.

Kyle Gillette is an associate professor of Human Communication and Theatre at Trinity University, Texas, U.S.A.

THE INVISIBLE CITY

Travel, Attention, and Performance

Kyle Gillette

LONDON AND NEW YORK

First published 2020
by Routledge
2 Park Square, Milton Park, Abingdon, Oxon OX14 4RN

and by Routledge
52 Vanderbilt Avenue, New York, NY 10017

Routledge is an imprint of the Taylor & Francis Group, an informa business

© 2020 Kyle Gillette

The right of Kyle Gillette to be identified as author of this work has been asserted by him in accordance with sections 77 and 78 of the Copyright, Designs and Patents Act 1988.

All rights reserved. No part of this book may be reprinted or reproduced or utilised in any form or by any electronic, mechanical, or other means, now known or hereafter invented, including photocopying and recording, or in any information storage or retrieval system, without permission in writing from the publishers.

Trademark notice: Product or corporate names may be trademarks or registered trademarks, and are used only for identification and explanation without intent to infringe.

British Library Cataloguing-in-Publication Data
A catalogue record for this book is available from the British Library

Library of Congress Cataloging-in-Publication Data
Names: Gillette, Kyle, 1979– author.
Title: The invisible city: travel, attention and performance / Kyle Gillette.
Description: Abingdon, Oxon; New York, NY: Routledge, 2020. | Includes bibliographical references and index.
Identifiers: LCCN 2019055884 (print) | LCCN 2019055885 (ebook) | ISBN 9780367133979 (hbk) | ISBN 9780367134006 (pbk) | ISBN 9780429026218 (ebk)
Subjects: LCSH: Space (Architecture)–Psychological aspects. | Cities and towns–Psychological aspects.
Classification: LCC NA2765 .G55 2020 (print) | LCC NA2765 (ebook) | DDC 720.1/03–dc23
LC record available at https://lccn.loc.gov/2019055884
LC ebook record available at https://lccn.loc.gov/2019055885

ISBN: 978-0-367-13397-9 (hbk)
ISBN: 978-0-367-13400-6 (pbk)
ISBN: 978-0-429-02621-8 (ebk)

Typeset in Bembo
by Newgen Publishing UK

CONTENTS

Acknowledgements		*vii*
Introduction		1
1	Thinking (with) the city	4
2	Writing (on) the city	18
3	Performing (in) the city	24
4	Cities and dreams: San Francisco	32
5	Cities and memory: Fara in Sabina	35
6	Invisible cities 1	39
7	Cities and speed: Tokyo	51
8	Cities and secrets: Paris	53
9	Invisible cities 2	57
10	Cities and violence: Rome	62
11	Cities and deception: Las Vegas	68

12 Invisible cities 3   72

13 Cities and empire: London   84

14 Cities and desire: Singapore   88

15 Invisible cities 4   92

16 Directions   96

Appendix: never the same river twice   *109*
Index   *130*

ACKNOWLEDGEMENTS

This book literally took a village: the village of Fara in Sabina, but also many colleagues, students, friends, partners, institutions, and foundations. I owe its inspiration and much of its content to Teatro Potlach, particularly the director Pino Di Buduo, co-founder Daniela Regnoli, actress Nathalie Mentha, company members Zsofia Gulyas and Irene Rossi, and regular collaborators Vincenzo Sansone, Marcus Acuan, Gustavo Riondet, and new partners Debora Columba and Stefano Cane. Other artists who have worked on *Invisible Cities* and workshops associated with the Festival Laboratorio Interculturale di Pratiche Teatrali played a vital role in forming my interest in the city's deep significance to theatre and culture: Julia Varley, Eugenio Barba, Keiin Yoshimura, Parvathy Baul, Claudio De Maglio, Bawa Iwayan, and Chintan Pandya. Sayna Ghaderi's photographs have deeply enriched these pages.

Over the course of three summers, student research assistants have helped me interview artists, workshop participants, and spectators; learn from archives; parse scholarly and literary sources; and think through intricate connections between theatre and the city: Leah Woehr, Holly Gabelmann, Nico Champion, Beverly Morabito (whose illustrations appear here), and Alexis Jarrett. The travel and labour for these assistants' work were made possible through generous fellowships granted by the Mellon Foundation. Roberto Prestigiacomo, a colleague who introduced me to Teatro Potlach's *Invisible Cities,* joined me for two journeys to Fara in Sabina. Other colleagues helped bring the group to Trinity University: Stacey Connelly, Tim Francis, Jodi Karjala, Andrew Hansen, and Lupita Puente. My colleagues in classics, Thomas Jenkins and Tim O'Sullivan, helped through conversations about cities and theatre both ancient and modern. I am grateful to Trinity University for providing financial support, an academic leave, and faculty development stipends for research on this book, and to Jane and the late Arthur Stieren and the Stieren Arts Enrichment Series who funded Teatro Potlach's production at Trinity. I am grateful for thoughtful riffing on these ideas with the editor Ben Piggott and exploring the early seeds of the book with old graduate school friends—particularly Kris Salata, Daniel Sack, and Rachel Anderson. A conversation with Peggy Phelan helped me think through the way the book's cities intersect with specific contemporary performances. More than anyone, I owe much of the thought of this book to countless conversations about cities and performance with my partner, spouse, colleague, and artistic collaborator Rachel Joseph, who introduced me to Italo Calvino's novel *Invisible Cities* and has been my fellow traveller ever since.

INTRODUCTION

Travelling through cities, I have been entranced by labyrinthine alleyways and glimpses of strangers' daily lives. But while I have tried to walk attentively, I have remained blind to deeper rhythms. I have pursued meanings that always seemed to recede around the next corner or behind closed doors. I have usually failed to see the labour that underlies cities' daily operations, except where infrastructure breaks down (pipes bursting, hard-hat-clad workers jackhammering sidewalks). I have spent time in Chinatown and Little India in Singapore but missed historical tensions between colonialism and immigration that have shaped each neighbourhood. I have sensed vague hauntings in Krakow and New Orleans but failed to feel the remembered (and forgotten) dead whose lives leave the most palpable but cryptic traces. I have walked the banks of the Tiber, the Seine, and the Thames without recognizing them for what they are: the very arteries that underlie and make their cities possible.

Yet, while encountering certain works of art, I have sometimes experienced compelling insights into hidden urban forces. Scenes from Yasujiro Ozu's *Tokyo Story* (1953) and Federico Fellini's *La Dolce Vita* (1960) project themselves onto apartment buildings as I walk down streets I have seen before on screen. My experience of cities is often startled awake by visual art displayed in urban museums like the Tate Modern or embedded provocatively in the streets—public sculptures by Louise Bourgeois or Ai Weiwei, street art by Banksy. Theatre has a particularly public power to reveal invisible forces and has for millennia forged strong ties to particular cities' identities, from the Theatre of Dionysus to the Beijing Opera and Berliner Ensemble. When I have experienced certain site-specific performances—notably, Spell#7's *Desire Paths* in Singapore and Teatro Potlach's *Invisible Cities* in Fara in Sabina—I have felt my travels extended and refined, layered with rich encounters between urban rhythms and singular details. Not only is the city fundamental as artistic site and source, a traveller might most vividly engage a city through its performances.

This book, *The Invisible City*, explores urban spaces from the perspective of a traveller, writer, and creator of theatre. It is about the unseen city, the hidden city—as experienced in transit, imagined in literature, and invoked through performance. The journey that follows traffics with many fellow travellers, but two are particularly significant guides: Italo Calvino's novel *Invisible Cities*, wherein Marco Polo describes cities to the Mongol emperor Kublai Khan, and Teatro Potlach's ongoing 27-year-old immersive, site-specific performance project by the same name, directed by Pino Di Buduo. *The Invisible City* is not about *Invisible Cities*—Calvino's or Potlach's—but it is after the same elusive stuff: the city below the visible surface or hidden within the surface itself. From Calvino, this book derives its deepest well of meanings associated with the city as imagined by travellers. *The Invisible City*'s structure is inspired by Calvino's novel, intermixing specific descriptions of cities with dialogue and theoretical considerations about the nature of urban space. This book also offers a close-up look at Teatro Potlach's eponymous performance based on Calvino's novel staged in dozens of cities internationally, from Mazatlán to Tehran. I consider the stakes and intercultural dynamics of Di Buduo's dramaturgy as city streets turn inside out, showing culture and labour normally obscured by architecture and habit.

The first chapters explore cities' cultural stakes, especially as explored in literature and performance. From Plato to Freud to Solnit, the city has appeared as a microcosm for civilization, a macrocosm for the individual, and a nexus of mysterious desires threading layers of public and private memory. These introductory pages hinge in part on the figure of the urban traveller—who, like the performer, or spectator, creates space through action and attention, seeking in cities both what they mean to show and what they work to conceal. By considering the role of cities in modern culture, especially literature and theatre, the opening chapters refine questions that animate the rest of the book: how does the act of travelling through cities connect to the act of writing, performing, or experiencing art? How might one meaningfully understand urban life as performance, or urban performances as grounded in the act of travel? Tourism often contorts cities into theatrical versions of themselves; how do performances that cast spectators into the position of travellers harness, resist, or complicate that theatricality? Some parts of cities become hidden by habitual systems such as the workaday commute or broader patterns of immigration and displacement. How might artists or travellers uniquely see beneath these blinding habits?

Much of this book develops these questions through a sustained consideration of Teatro Potlach's performance *Invisible Cities* and the ways it works to unveil hidden myths and memories of the cities it embeds itself within. Drawing from performances I have experienced as a spectator and collaborator from 2015 to 2019, I unpack the experience of travelling through its worlds and consider the group's efforts to excavate invisible urban memories by fusing the role of spectator and traveller. Through four years of archival research, interviews, observation, and participation, I have come to appreciate the complex urban anthropology the director Pino Di Buduo guides through Teatro Potlach's work. While the group has performed this piece in dozens of cities since 1992, these pages draw particular attention to four performances in Potlach's home village Fara in Sabina, where the performance originated.

Interwoven with this consideration of Teatro Potlach's *Invisible Cities*, several vignettes unfold cities that have for various reasons absorbed me as a traveller in that particular way the act of urban travel often seems to become a form of theatre. As a spectator and participant, I have found in the cities I recall certain theatrical dynamics related to memory, haunting, dreams, and invisibility. These vignettes of cities depict urban forces filtered through my remembered cities: recollections of traversing streets and witnessing events that hint at the invisible lurking within the everyday. Like the cities Marco Polo describes to Kublai Khan in Calvino's *Invisible Cities*, these are partial, perhaps largely imagined or displaced, memories of cities I've been to, no doubt intermixed over time. But also like those invisible cities throughout Khan's dying empire, these observations point to invisible elements intrinsic to cities as such.

The final chapter of the book, 'Directions,' offers prompts for readers interested in engaging cities as artist-travellers. I have developed these exercises from 2006 to 2019, in classes and workshops I have created at Stanford University, the American Conservatory Theater, and Trinity University, and most recently in a workshop called 'Cities of Memory,' I lead in Fara in Sabina as part of Teatro Potlach's annual intercultural performance festival (Festival Laboratorio Interculturale di Pratiche Teatrali). Some of these exercises have played a role in developing material for 2018 and 2019 performances of *Invisible Cities* too, and as such, turn the book's scope from the outside to the inside of the performance. I have developed most of these workshops separately from that context, but in every situation taught them in order to guide participants to create texts, site-specific performances, and videos that arise from their urban research. These prompts are designed to help tease out the encounter between travel and performance in ways that artists can draw from to help research cities, whether for content or as a formal stimulus to hone attention, experience, memory, and imagination. The questions accordingly grow more practical in this part: Where can the work of particularly mindful, present travellers—as they experience the world through intimate physical and mental engagement, creating space through movement and attention—feed the work of performers and writers? How might focusing on the concrete experiences of travelling through cities help develop a theatre or film director's specificity and imaginative depth? How can site-specific performances in cities inform the work of novelists, poets, film-makers, painters, installation artists, curators, festival planners, tour guides, and others who draw from or create within a city? These 'Directions' also frame how imaginative work can help anyone who wishes to travel with greater meaning and care—whether they embark on foreign adventures or seek to revisit well-worn pathways with fresh eyes.

1
THINKING (WITH) THE CITY

The city has long played a foundational role in western culture's performances of myth, justice, and power. Over six millennia ago in Mesopotamia, Uruk became the world's first true city, the birthplace of writing and stone architecture. The ancient Sumerian city later garnered poetic fame as its quasi-mythic king Gilgamesh starred in the world's oldest extant epic. In the *Iliad*, Homer sang of Troy and the war outside its walls. In the *Odyssey*, he sang of long journeys home afterwards. Centuries later, Aeschylus's ancient trilogy the *Oresteia* begins with the return of Agamemnon after conquering Troy and slaughtering or enslaving its citizens. In the first play, Clytemnestra murders her husband Agamemnon in revenge for the sacrifice of their daughter; in the second, Orestes murders his mother Clytemnestra. In the trilogy's final play, Aeschylus creates a utopian image of the democratic city Athens to replace archaic blood feuds and monarchies with civic justice determined by a jury. Orestes' murder of his mother—and the generational net of retribution around his vengeful act—threatens the community beyond the cursed House of Atreus: this web of violence hinders progress more generally towards a public and deliberative *polis* by making it difficult for citizens to trust in safe civic space. Tribal blood feuds, with their clannish infanticidal or matricidal acts and endless acts of revenge, must be replaced, sublimated into the progressive Athenian vision of civilization. Hence a city on a hill where courtrooms replace battlefields, democracy replaces tyranny, and theatres replace fortresses.[1]

During the City Dionysia Festival so fundamental to classical Athenian identity, in the Theatre of Dionysus embedded in the heart of the city, Aeschylus staged a mythic Athens as the embodiment of democracy, the triumph of classical urban deliberation over tribal affiliations (and of Athena's patriarchal allegiance to Zeus over old pre-Olympian gods and their chthonic matriarchal roots beyond city walls). Athena and the jury transform the vengeful Furies into harmonious

FIGURE 1.1 Drawing by Beverly Morabito

Eumenides who swear to nourish the city and its citizens forever. At the end of the trilogy, chorus, tragedians, and audience progress out of the open air theatre, into the city. Aeschylus' trilogy, at least mythically, cultivated earth and old tribal energies into democratic urban flourishing. Wealthy citizens funded and performed the plays that competed in the City Dionysia Festival, ostensibly as devotional acts to Dionysus, thus infusing the theatrical with the political and religious status of the city. Sharing images, stories, and discourse publicly, the ancient Greek theatre thus imagined the city as a site where citizens participate in the same spectacle, the same myths whereby Athens can negotiate shared civic identity.

6 Thinking (with) the city

In part as a reaction against the democratic and theatrical character of Athens, Plato took the ancient Greek *polis* as a helpful model through which to imagine more clearly the interrelated parts of the individual mind, or soul. Through the character of his mentor Socrates, Plato imagines the hypothetical city of his *Republic* as a way to show why it is better for a person to be just than unjust, better to pursue wisdom than to remain blinded by appearances—even though unjust people and those intoxicated by images can all too often appear more successful or comfortably entertained. Injustice and delusion, threats to anyone's character, and therefore happiness, grow more apparent when magnified to the size of a city—here, interrelated parts of society reveal how injustice and imbalance cause suffering. Suspicious of Athens' democratic institutions and theatrical fictions, Plato imagined a city ruled instead by properly educated philosophers, guided by rational inquiry and clear thinking. His city would be organized around the Truth as understood abstractly: ideal Forms outside time, not prone to mutable opinions of the pleasure-seeking populace and its theatrical depictions of social relations. So should the ideal citizen be ruled, Plato's Socrates reasoned: by looking for the source of the light, by a desire to understand the deepest nature of reality and ethics, not by getting caught up in sensory images and seductive stories. The ideal Forms of heaven transcend not only artistic depictions but even concrete particulars that litter city streets—things themselves being mere copies, imperfect, all too mutable.[2]

Plato's ideal truth cannot be found in the tragic fictions of Aeschylus shared in a city theatre. These deceptive images, as Plato saw it, were just so many shadows projected on a wall of the cave, seductively confusing spectators about their veracity. If Aeschylus' theatre offered images, mythic figures, and patriotic narratives, it still left humankind in the dark, no better than cave-dwellers; it still left citizen-spectators just as blind to the nature of things. From prehistoric Lascaux cave paintings to Plato's allegorical cave, was civilization to remain stunted at this primitive illusionistic phase, still walled off in self-imposed artifice, dripping with superstition, emotional manipulation, and magical thinking? Plato's ideal city would invert the cave's darkness and dissimulation, drawing citizens into the light. The theatre, like the cave, would have to be left behind (or radically transformed) for a balanced city, for a balanced citizen. Athens invisibly underlies Plato's ideal city in photonegative: the dangerous public sphere of theatrical space, spectacle, sophistic opinion-peddling, and democratic speeches. Yet Athens also provided locations for Socrates to question sophists and challenge young aristocrats to examine their assumptions. (This city eventually provided the jury that 'democratically' condemned Socrates to death for corrupting the youth.) Plato founded his Academy, where he staged lectures and dialectic philosophical inquiry on the outskirts of the city, just beyond Athens' ancient walls.

Centuries later, St. Augustine of Hippo built on top of Plato's ideas to conceive his influential *City of God*, which contrasted the 'Earthly City' of Pagan Rome against the divine joy and harmony of a 'Celestial City.' The City of God, where divine worship spills out of church buildings into pure city streets populated by the elect, brings cloistered ritual into public performance and resembles a vision of urban flourishing imaginable to Roman citizens of late antiquity but idealized into an ur-city of pure spirit, one that operates in direct opposition to the moral decay (violence, pleasure, riches, decadence, and debauched theatricality) of the 'Earthly City.' As Rome was sacked, Augustine argued against those who blamed the young religion, Visigoths spared churches, where providence protected the only aspect of Rome worth saving: its nascent Christian community.[3] Against a backdrop of Roman comedy's harsh satirical depictions of Christians—and more violent entertainments involving torture by fire, lions, and crucifixion—the early church shared Plato's distaste for theatre proper and also the city's paratheatrical entertainments. Early church fathers shared the ancient philosopher's scepticism of urban pleasures.

Despite its bloody circuses, persecuting emperors, and capacity for sinfulness as depicted in the Hebrew scriptures (Sodom and Gomorrah), the city also provided Christians concrete ways to imagine heaven and a renewed significance to Jerusalem. Cities' interaction across cultures and languages made possible the religion's first centuries. City names came to shape the founding documents of the New Testament: the Letters of Paul to churches in Corinth, Galatia, Ephesus, Philippi, Colossae, Thessalonica, and, of course, Rome. Rome itself continued after the ascendancy of Christianity as the state religion under Constantine to make of its streets elaborate displays of objects, animals, human beings, and cultural performances sacked from conquered cities. Within a few centuries, collections from across the former empire and beyond not only filled private villas and public piazzas, but especially the endless galleries of the Vatican Museums: galleries of objects that witness to and perform global imperial power culturally and financially long after the fall of the western empire. The church, meanwhile, gave birth to liturgical dramas that spilled into city streets across Europe, nourishing the very theatre early church fathers once decried as satanic. The medieval church's architectural and theatrical work tried to stage the invisible city, the celestial city, in the very streets of the mortal city, the temporal city: Oberammergau, York, Avila.

Western literature's visions of paradise or the infernal are deeply interwoven with theatrical visions of the city. In the European medieval imagination, celestial realms often appeared urban in their population density and elaborate fantastical architecture or arrangements of bodies on successive levels, from the seven-walled city of Heaven filled with beautiful perfume and music in the Irish poem *Vision of Adamnán* to the city of Dis in the sixth circle of Dante's *Inferno*. Renaissance popes and nobles spent vast fortunes on building Vatican City and Florence into open, well-planned heavens on earth (even as powerful families like the Borgias and Medici created illicit cities hiding in plain sight or behind hallowed doors). Theatre, processions, and spectacles played an important role in these urban displays of divinity and debauchery. Protestant theocratic cities such as John Calvin's Geneva and Oliver Cromwell's London banished theatre and celebratory public festivals, associating these modes of performance with the ritualistic, latently pagan, and theatrical cities of Roman Catholicism. Jewish culture and thought flourished—though often under terrible persecution—in neighbourhoods in Rome, Krakow, Amsterdam, and

Cordoba where synagogues, theatres, and literary and intellectual life wrote the ongoing history of the people outside Jerusalem. Jerusalem stands, of course, at the nexus of the three Abrahamic faiths, a city traumatized by millennia of sacking and pregnant with meaning for most of the world's population. Before Mecca, Jerusalem was the first Qibla, the Islamic holy city all the faithful prayed towards.

The theological significance of cities is hardly restricted to monotheistic or western traditions. Buddhism, though associated with Thai forest monasteries, Tibetan mountains, and Indian deer parks, flourished through its dissemination in cities, as Hinduism had already thrived on the populated banks of the Ganges. Shinto shrines and Zen temples are deeply interwoven with the urban aesthetic of old Japanese cities like Kyoto even as they idealize monastic life outside cities. Confucian rules govern not only filial piety and civic behaviour but also the geometric arrangement of Beijing's Forbidden City and related holy sites. Confucianism regulates city life—political, familial, architectural, and bureaucratic relations—with great ritual care that keeps things in harmony with traditional modes of authority. Even Taoism, associated as it is with rivers and secluded mountains, informs urban design practices through feng shui concepts. Taoist priests and laity memorialize the dead in elaborate temples from Taipei to Hong Kong; funerals fill the streets outside temples with rich singing, colourful costumes, dances, incense, and ritualized mourning practices.

Religions, though so many originate in deserts and forests, become themselves most theatrically in cities: Bodhgaya, Lhasa, Kyoto, Varanasi, Mecca, Jerusalem, Cairo, the Vatican. It is in cities that religion's processions and architecture most vividly sanctify everyday space, bringing invisible ghosts into daily life. But religions often eschew cities too, retreating to caves and beneath trees to find God, or goddesses, or enlightenment. Monasteries offer alternatives to the city's seductive, excessive ways, working salvation by offering an alternative to urban life. The rhythms of Benedictine and Shaolin monastic orders alike tend to those whose suffering magnified in cities. Then again, religions of the desert or mountains often imagine an ideal or promised city, a Kalapa or Jerusalem. Within or outside the city, organized religions rarely ignore the city. Like a secular pilgrim, I gravitate towards sacred spaces when I travel, seeing in temple architecture and devotional ritual performances particularly theatrical expressions of the world's religions, shadows of the city.

Secular modern thought often examines cities as microcosms that stage civilization's political or psychological ills. Karl Marx's experiences and research in London helped shape his understanding of bourgeois capitalism's alienating effects on the factory-bound proletariat. In the following century, cities from Paris to Moscow would become the epicentres of revolutionary acts inspired by his writings. For Sigmund Freud, Rome offered an imperfect but influential model for the individual psyche, with its ruins of previous stages built upon and sublimated into new structures:

> let us make the fantastic supposition that Rome were not a human dwelling-place, but a mental entity with just as long and varied a past history: that is, in which nothing once constructed had perished, and all the earlier stages

of development had survived alongside the latest. This would mean that in Rome the palaces of the Caesars were still standing on the Palatine and the Septizonium of Septimius Severus was still towering to its old height; that the beautiful statues were still standing in the colonnade of the Castle of St. Angelo, as they were up to its siege by the Goths, and so on. […] on the Piazza of the Pantheon we should find out only the Pantheon of today as bequeathed to us by Hadrian, but on the same site also Agrippa's original edifice; indeed, the same ground would support the church of Santa Maria sopra Minerva and the old temple over which it was built.[4]

Rome has always had to grow atop and through reappropriated broken remains. Between major disasters like sacking and civil war, Rome crumbled through more everyday entropy caused by urban development and weather; it was restored, rebuilt, transformed, and still bears the scars of its mutations. Were its architectural and historical developments to coexist spatially at once they would come close to the way psychic space works for Freud. Rome, like any city, is a palimpsest, not only of architecture, but also of centuries upon centuries of biographical details, speeches, parades, fashions, street foods, each new cultural layer covering over what came before—but incompletely; traces remain, bleeding between sediments.[5] In habits, architectural features, styles of dress and walking, traces remain. An analogous psychic return is true for Freud's unconscious layers of the individual subject, and even civilization itself: our earliest structures of consciousness and drives lie invisible but ever-present within our daily lives, sublimated by later developments but never completely displaced. Prior worlds persist in civilization's cultural practices and languages, its patriarchal religious icons, whose repression of older epochs and archaic drives is necessary to keep us from constantly killing or mating with each other long enough to build cities, but this repression has consequences, or 'discontents.' For theorists influenced by Jacques Lacan, whose re-readings of Freud brought structuralism to bear on psychoanalytic thought, the city resembles an enigmatic text or collection of signifying chains, its inaccessible, traumatic Real always displaced by tantalizing images, libidinal economies: advertisements, restaurants, domestic interior designs, secret cruising spots.

Aggressively modern cities can expand horizons even as they trample the past, constantly recreating the subject through urban reinvention. As Michel de Certeau notes, New York City is quite unlike Rome in at least this respect:

> New York has never learned the art of growing old by playing on all its pasts. Its present invents itself, from hour to hour, in the act of throwing away its previous accomplishments and challenging the future. A city composed of paroxysmal places in monumental reliefs. The spectator can read in it a universe that is constantly exploding.[6]

New York suggests not just a microcosm for the universe as explosive and ever-changing but also a macrocosm for the sort of citizen ready to leave behind provincial hometowns or ancestral roots in favour of struggle, radical renewal, and mutable identity: immigrants from Newark to Nanjing, would-be entrepreneurs, singers, actors, dancers, performance artists, professors, editors, writers, bankers, stockbrokers, politicians, activists, critics, graduate students. As Jack Kerouac notes, back from his trip immortalized in *On the Road*, there is a manic rush to the city that concentrates ambition and striving:

> the absolute madness and fantastic hoorair of New York with its millions and millions hustling forever for a buck among themselves, the mad dream—grabbing, taking, giving, sighing, dying, just so they could be buried in those awful cemetery cities beyond Long Island City.[7]

New York suggests a distinctively striving kind of citizen, a certain openly daring version of human being, but one whose manic patterns close citizens off from the outside world and deeper rhythms of the earth. New York suggests a particularly modern vision of social order: experimental, competitive, capitalist, multicultural, always under construction.

Cities like New York—or Mumbai, Buenos Aires, Cape Town—showcase limit-cases that experiment at the edges of economic and technological possibility. Take those ultra-modern cities that stretch to the sky: Tokyo, Dubai, Shanghai. Or the rough neighbourhoods that magnify poverty by contrasting it against outrageous wealth: the favelas of Rio de Janeiro, the slums of Nairobi, or once heroin-plagued parts of Edinburgh. These cities cry out for social reform, for novelistic or cinematic depictions that show what lies repressed beneath each city's advertised self-image. There are ancient cities, like Carthage or Babylon, haunted by vanished civilizations, and the practically newborn, like Gujarat International Finance Tec-City, that may prophesy technocratic futures. As the 2019 Los Angeles setting of Ridley Scott's 1982 film *Blade Runner* passes into recent history, its once-futurist sentient android replicants and ecological catastrophes—not to mention Japanese noodle shops, mythic corporate pyramids and decaying 'modern' buildings—increasingly resemble a recognizable postmodern city of late capitalism. Metropolises can stage forces of capitalism, communism, and fascism with a degree of concentration that would necessarily be more diluted in suburbs and countrysides. Cities at their most developed offer a well-funded apparatus that can include elaborate parades, propaganda, and police forces.

Various kinds of cities—modern, postmodern, utopian, dystopian, ancient, mysterious, chaotic, master-planned—tend to overlap in the same city. Above, the skyscrapers; below, the ghettos. Circulating the business districts: novelty and experiments in social relations; around the centre: palatial exaggerations of authoritarian control. (Recessed behind alleyways and beneath church floors: the remembered or forgotten dead.) Each city-within-the-city remains mostly blind to the other cities that it interpenetrates, that interpenetrate it. When I walk or ride public transportation, I sometimes feel that I catch glimpses through thin membranes that separate worlds, catching peeks of other, invisible cities. But this sense of contact has always been fleeting and partial. Travelling through the city connects me intimately to the urban fabric but as it immerses me it simultaneously blinds me. As de Certeau notes in his influential essay 'Walking in the City,' the 'act of walking' is comparable to speech in its performative nature, 'a spatial acting-out of the place (just as the speech act is an acoustic acting-out of language).'[8] The city only exists, or comes to be, through the activity of its people. But pedestrians participate in a network of meanings, traffic flows, economies, actions, encounters, and images they mostly cannot see: other people, private lives going on behind closed doors, boulevards of potential experiences just around the corner, hidden infrastructure, demographic patterns, energy usage. If the city is like a language, it is one that hides, renders invisible, its grammar to those who perform it into being (and are in turn created by the city). De Certeau contrasts the walker's street-level view against the panoptic distance afforded from the top of the World Trade Center, one that gives the illusion both of power and of absolute legibility: laying the streets out along a grid below. Pedestrians are blinded by proximity and possibility: so many streets and shops and theatres, so much life one can never see or know.

In this sense, the modern city can stage a vibrant public sphere in its cafes even as it fosters radical individualism (and loneliness) in its streets, apartments, and trams.[9] Each person in the city engages in daily acts of being (working, commuting, eating, wandering, exchanging goods and currency, interacting with friends and strangers) made possible but simultaneously rendered invisible by the city, as Alfie Bown notes. Writing psychoanalytically about the city in literature, Bown depicts 'the everyday' as 'the city's unconscious, something elusive and impossible to pin down but something under whose influence we live.'[10] That unconscious dimension of the city directly shapes 'the individual of today,' who 'is engulfed within' the city 'and yet simultaneously deprived' of its legible meaning. The city 'is equally inescapable and unreadable, constructing us but refusing to confess how.'[11] The labyrinthine complexity of the city, the layered texture of its everyday lives, makes it invisible in part by habituating citizens to pay the most myopic attention to their particular paths: home, work, school, shops. The modern city in particular, as David Clarke notes, represents 'the world as experienced by the stranger, and the experience of a world populated by strangers.'[12] City-dwellers do not see each other, cut off, alienated.

But the ways city-dwellers fail to see—each other or the deeper rhythms of urban life—unfold within daily lives inundated with images of other lives. People's mutual separation is not for lack of visibility; it has to do with the way city-dwellers see brief, revealing but ultimately fragmentary peeks into each other's routines, even those within the home. Like Jeffries in Alfred Hitchcock's 1954 film *Rear Window*, urban dwellers do see startlingly intimate details of other people living their lives, but out of context, in fragments, and in a way filtered through narcissistic projections, conditioned by personal experiences, private desires, memories. Being surrounded by people whose everyday lives are on display—and who in turn can watch you back—can produce greater alienation rather than familiarity, never mind intimacy. Olivia Laing notes how seeing strangers across the street through

12 Thinking (with) the city

FIGURE 1.2 Strangers in transit; photo by Sayna Ghaderi

apartment windows in New York amplified her loneliness when she first moved to the city:

> This is the thing about cities, the way that even indoors you're always at the mercy of a stranger's gaze. Wherever I went—pacing back and forth between the bed and couch; roaming into the kitchen to regard the abandoned boxes of ice cream in the freezer—I could be seen by the people who lived in the Arlington, the vast Queen Anne co-op that dominated the view, its ten brick storeys lagged in scaffolding. At the same time, I could also play the watcher, *Rear Window*-style, peering in on dozens of people with whom I'd never exchange a word, all of them engrossed in the small intimacies of the day. Loading a dishwasher naked; tapping in on heels to cook the children's supper.[13]

Laing's book *The Lonely City* examines the loneliness at the heart of her first-hand experience, but also unpacks how urban loneliness has shaped the life and work of Edward Hopper, Andy Warhol, and Henry Darger. The everyday dimension of private behaviours framed by windows across the street cuts off potential encounters between individuals, preventing intimate contact, simultaneously creating provocative scenes and objectifying fellow citizens—wrapping them up in suspicion, prurient intrigue, the male gaze, and all manner of fantasy. Considering this framing aesthetically, by discussing it theoretically or literally using it to make art, may show spectators just how blind people are to the depth and reach of others' experience. Apartment dwellers in New York are all too often, like the twenty-first-century residents of the developed world more generally, mutually alienated spectators, mediated through screens ranging from windows to smartphones. While this mediated dynamic can cut citizens off from each other, making it difficult to form authentic traditional communities particular to less urban contexts, it can also generate aesthetic insights if glimpsed, as Laing suggests, through the eyes of the traveller—who, for her, is deeply connected to the figure of the artist. The traveller, the citizen's inverted doppelgänger, can recognize and then recall traces of the city through solitary observation and imagination, breaking free of local habituation. The artist-as-traveller seeks to bridge the gap erected by mediation and isolation, bringing lives into deeper contact and helping make the invisible visible.

Artists such as Hopper, Warhol, and Darger may harness the solitude imposed by urban encounters in order to frame the world anew. But loneliness is no guarantee of aesthetic liberation or imaginative connections across the chasm of alienation. Nor is getting out of the house necessarily a balm to loneliness. Outside individual apartment windows, daily life unfolds on the streets, where another sort of solitude or solipsism dominates even among thick crowds of people. Commuters often grow blind to each other through rote habit, following fixed routes from home to work to grocery store with little variation or thought of others, except perhaps defensive thoughts, thoughts of survival and fear that do little to encourage open encounters with strangers who cross paths. Bourgeois professionals walk by the homeless without glancing down much. Latina, Asian, black, and white people routinely live side by side in multi-ethnic or adjacent neighbourhoods without associating deeply. Residents, even if fairly new to the city, often find themselves blinded by workaday motives related to economic activity; thus forces of production subsume otherwise singular details of experience into going to work or spending its compensatory pay on weekends. Commercial and political interests shape pathways for city dwellers and travellers alike; corporations and city bureaucrats exercise invisibly manipulative or openly coercive control of routes between and access to different areas. They censor and shape what enters the visible horizon of the city.

Yet certain ways of travelling the city may help reveal invisible forces. Beginning in the 1950s, revolutionary poets and proto-punk intellectuals of the Situationist International led by Guy Debord took to the streets of Paris for an influential but originally subversive Situationist practice, the *dérive* (or drift), wherein

> one or more persons during a certain period drop their relations, their work and leisure activities, and all their other usual motives for movement and action, and let themselves be drawn by the attractions of the terrain and the encounters they find there.[14]

Cities have 'psychogeographical' contours, with 'constant currents, fixed points and vortexes that strongly discourage entry into or exit from certain zones.'[15] As Bown puts it, the dérive is 'about showing the subject how the city has an unconscious that organizes and controls its inhabitants.'[16] The Situationists walked to unfold the city's unconscious drives, its underlying unity, liberated from routine or economic purpose; they tried to become, through their walking, more insightful spectators, emancipated subjects who could see the hidden city normally obscured beneath purpose-driven commutes or shopping itineraries. At the same time, Situationists wanted to become revolutionary actors, citizens who actualize the city's latent contours. They sought to bring about a flourishing of community as made possible by the city yet repressed by forces of government control or consumer capitalism.

The Situationist dérive seems to rely on a sense that cities are like art, or that their most interesting possibilities can be actualized through pseudo-artistic activities. Debord was not the first, of course, to approach Paris this way. In the nineteenth century, the *flâneur* was a paradigmatic literary figure: the spectator-traveller who strolls along the boulevard, making of the city an aesthetic experience. Charles Baudelaire's poems written from long walks through Paris streets suggest a way to curate all the sights, sounds, and smells of the city with a sense of artful attention. Baudelaire writes in his 1863 essay 'The Painter of Modern Life' that the flâneur's

> profession is to merge with the crowd. For the perfect idler, for the passionate observer it becomes an immense source of enjoyment to establish his dwelling in the throng, in the ebb and flow, the bustle, the fleeting and the infinite.[17]

In this sense that privileged traveller

> watches the river of life flow past him in all its splendour and majesty. He marvels at the eternal beauty and the amazing harmony of life in the capital cities, a harmony so providentially maintained amid the turmoil of human freedom.[18]

Walter Benjamin, writing in the early twentieth century, reads Baudelaire's texts as something like literary transubstantiations. They transform the potentially over-stimulating effects of urban modernity—loud vehicles, massive crowds of strangers, factory machines, display windows, advertising, speed—into poetry that transcends it, situating the traveller as the rightful heir of aristocratic leisure, a relative to the dandy or aesthete.

Baudelaire's poetry attends to and expresses the experience of the city such that it puts the subject undergoing this experience at the centre of the city's immersive performance. This poetic turn, or transformation of urban experience into art, obviates the desensitizing stimulus that shield city-dwellers might otherwise need to protect themselves from shocks to the mind and body. One possible response to the modern city's excessive stimuli is to grow callous and cruel, dulled to the world. Another is to succumb to anxiety. The subject imagined in Benjamin's reading of Baudelaire can become a member and even master of the modern world by getting lost in the throng—but only if the subject embraces the city with a particular quality of attention: the absolutely disinterested aesthetic condition of the consummate spectator and consummate artist in one. He (distinctively male for Baudelaire, not to mention physically capable of walking and financially capable of leisure time) internalizes the urban world by walking through it, even as he remained disinterested, an aesthete. The *flâneur* heralds the consumer capitalist, the bourgeois city-dweller, for whom city streets are transformed into an outdoor shopping mall. But the modern bourgeoisie later renders the *flâneur* obsolete by the ubiquitous theatricalization of urban experience catered to pleasure. The bourgeois stroller has gradually expanded to include others: women, immigrants, lesbian and gay tourists, people of multiple racial and ethnic backgrounds, even people with more limited mobility, though Paris, like many European cities, remains centred on the experience of able-bodied European heterosexual men, from steep stairways and buildings without lifts to burlesque entertainments of the Moulin Rouge and paintings of nude women in the Museé d'Orsay. Few accommodations are made for newcomers to the culturally sanctioned bourgeoisie, and those newcomers must perform their identity as part of this privileged group by adopting its dress, its habits of walking and talking. Occasionally an exception is made for those with disabilities, but only if they can perform their exceptional nature in a way that appeals to the bourgeois spectator: the 'Bubble Girl's' 1963 photo shoot in Paris, for example, her plexiglass sphere suspended by cranes in impossible locations—on the Seine, above a cafe.

Benjamin, inverting Baudelaire's privileged position, engaged the margins of bourgeois Paris as well as the arcades of the city: not only the products and display windows but also refuse, the detritus of bourgeois culture. In so doing, Benjamin recognized a fundamental doubleness to the urban traveller. Travelling between advertising posters and through curated streets and arcades, the bourgeois stroller absorbed cultural mandates and commodity fetishes through sensory experiences. But at the same time another kind of walker, the 'rag-picker' at the edge of culture, emerged: this figure explores mobility between the imagined and real city, the ancient and modern, between classes. The rag-picker can pick through the cast-off junk produced by industrial and consumer capitalism like a detective whose subject is the city itself:

> Here we have a man whose job it is to gather the day's refuse in the capital. Everything that the big city has thrown away, everything it has lost, everything it has scorned, everything it has crushed underfoot he catalogues and collects. He collates the annals of intemperance, the capharnaum of waste. He sorts things out and selects judiciously: he collects like a miser guarding a treasure, refuse which will assume the shape of useful or gratifying objects between the jaws of the goddess of Industry.[19]

The rag-picker becomes a subversive anthropologist of the bourgeoisie who detects the repressed operations of capitalism's insidious economies of desire. The rag-picker figure can sidestep officially sanctioned sidewalks or streets, transgressing boundaries and ducking beneath police tape or slipping behind abandoned buildings to see things increasingly invisible to most Parisians. Similarly, the rag-picker can evade the intoxicating pull of consumer displays (advertisements, corporate logos,

FIGURE 1.3 Cinema America in Trastevere, Rome; photo by Sayna Ghaderi

shop windows) that manipulate desire while obscuring the labour and natural world they exploit to produce goods and services. Benjamin's radical subversion, like Debord's, consists not in refusal to conform to routes through particular streets or through his accomplishment of particular politically/socially/economically productive tasks. The rag-picker, especially as developed into a writer or performer, threatens to see, and reveal, the invisible city.

Notes

1 Aeschylus, *The Oresteia*, trans. David Mulroy (University of Wisconsin Press, 2018).
2 Plato, *Republic*, trans. R.E. Allen (Yale University Press, 2006).
3 Augustine, *City of God Against the Pagans*, trans. R.W. Dyson (Cambridge University Press, 1998).
4 Sigmund Freud, *Civilization and Its Discontents*, trans. Joan Riviere (Dover, 1994), 6.
5 For a particularly thoughtful consideration of Freud's ideas on Rome as related to the work of urban travel and the theatre of Raffaello Sanzio, see Joe Kelleher, 'Falling Out of the World: In Rome with Freud, a Friend, Moses and Societas Raffaello Sanzio,' *Performance Research* 12.2 (June 2007).
6 Michel de Certeau, *The Practice of Everyday Life*, trans. Steven Rendall (University of California Press, 1984), 93.
7 Jack Kerouac, *On the Road* (Penguin, 2003), 107.
8 De Certeau, *Practice of Everyday Life*, 97–8.
9 See Jurgen Habermas, *The Structural Transformation of the Public Sphere*, trans. Frederick Lawrence (MIT Press, 1989).

10 Alfie Bown, *The Palgrave Handbook of Literature and the City*, ed. Jeremy Tambling (Palgrave, 2016), 75.
11 Ibid., 84.
12 Clarke, *Palgrave Handbook*, 4.
13 Olivia Laing, *The Lonely City* (Picador, 2016), 19.
14 Guy Debord, 'Theory of the Derive' (1958), in *Situationist International Anthology*, ed. Ken Knabb (Bureau of Public Secrets, 2012), 50–4.
15 Ibid.
16 Bown, *Palgrave Handbook*, 80.
17 Charles Baudelaire, *The Painter of Modern Life and Other Essays*, trans. Jonathan Mayne (Phaidon, 1965), 9.
18 Ibid., 11.
19 Walter Benjamin, *The Writer of Modern Life: Essays on Charles Baudelaire* (Harvard University Press, 2006), 108.

2
WRITING (ON) THE CITY

As Jeremy Tambling writes in his introduction to the *Palgrave Handbook of Literature and the City*, 'Being in the city expands being; the observer cannot remain outside the world which he or she reflects, and so gives back something to the crowd, in a constant exchange, a force field.'[1] Writers who focus on the city, like travellers, become inextricably caught up in the urban fabric while invoking it in words, both forming their literary structures in response to the city and leaving their words scrawled like graffiti on walls for future travellers to read—and scrawl over too. Ciudad Juarez's yawning chasm of murdered women thinly disguised as Santa Teresa in Roberto Bolaño's *2666*, the San Francisco of Solnit and Kerouac, the Paris of Baudelaire and Stein, Murakami's Tokyo, Kafka's Prague, Joyce's Dublin: cities draw writers into the pleasures, horrors, possibilities, and purposes of being and then bear the traces of writers' experiences.

Writing the experience of a city often drives readers towards journeys there, much as films and paintings can inspire viewers to take a trip. Alain de Botton shows in *The Art of Travel* how 'insofar as we travel in search of beauty, works of art may in small ways start to influence where we would like to travel to.'[2] A book or poem can also shape how readers experience those cities when they really go, priming travellers to engage its mysteries in particular ways. Note the rich cottage industry in tourist walks through Dickens' or Woolf's London. Even without a guide, to walk through Mayfair with the words of Clarissa Dalloway in your mind is to experience the very entwining of thought, memory, and sensory perception Woolf explores formally in her 1925 novel—a subjective position that expands and interpenetrates as it interweaves other minds, other perspectives, within continuous physical spaces. In cities, lives can burst out of private dwellings and engage each other through complex webs of interconnection that bring writers insights about what it means to be a person or part of a culture. Like Woolf's London, Joyce's Dublin both attracts and primes travellers, constructing the city as a desirable location connected not to its particularity as a site but as a paradigmatic stage whereupon the mindful traveller can see repetitions that reflect the great cyclical procession of history, its wavelike rhythms. *Ulysses*:

> Things go on same, day after day: squads of police marching out, back: trams in, out. [...] Cityful passing away, other cityful coming, passing away too: other coming on, passing on. Houses, lines of houses, streets, miles of pavements, piledup bricks, stones. Changing hands. This owner, that. Landlord never dies they say. Other steps into his shoes when he gets his notice to quit. They buy the place up with gold and still they have all the gold.[3]

In his 2011 novel *Open City*, Teju Cole gets at New York's multiple overlapping layers of displacement and immigration through his Nigerian protagonist's attentive ambulations through Manhattan: he sees traces of cultures and history apparent in architectural relics and traffic patterns, in singular details that add up to tangible contrasts between places:

> Each neighborhood of the city appeared to be made of a different substance, each seemed to have a different air pressure, a different psychic weight: the bright lights and shuttered shops, the housing projects and luxury hotels, the fire escapes and city parks.[4]

The rhythm of buses and birds, the relentless cycles of ethnic displacements, and the walker's individual train of thoughts offer Cole, like Woolf, Joyce, Kerouac, and many other writers, richly textured and self-contained miniature worlds. Cities have a special capacity to provoke the literary imagination, offering alternative versions of the world and richly layered systems of signs, fields of social relations within which to expand and tease out human being: the meaningful and meaningless repetitions of modern but also ancient history, the ruins of economic exploitation, the way individual consciousnesses wrestle with patterns passed down through generations.

How can the modern novel know people at the individual, social, or historical level, Jeremy Tambling asks, 'when the city becomes full of atomized groups who do not know each other?'[5] What would it even mean for writers (or citizens generally) to know each other when the experiences and choices that constitute identity blur and shift in response to rapid urban rhythms? The modern city establishes a laboratory of experience from which the modernist novel emerges, composed as it is by 'moments and chance happenings, inconsequential in themselves but, in their immensely multiple totality, composing city life as experience rather than biography.'[6] Biography presupposes a cohesive, continuous understanding of self, a pre-existing subject who lives *through* and *in* cities, growing and changing but without losing a certain characteristic thread of identity. Nineteenth-century novels in Russia, Britain, and the United States often depicted realistic urban details as backdrops for a character's rise to or fall from grace, or as a technique to offer obstacles that help display social problems. From Fyodor Dostoevsky to Charles Dickens and Theodore Dreiser, cities are important but distinct from the characters who inhabit them—they are, rather, settings for biographical events to unfold. For Woolf or Joyce, on the other hand, who depict 'city life as experience rather than biography,' the traveller's consciousness swirls through sensory and signifying phenomena, experiencing the memory of the city as invisibly repeated through everyday action. Experience surrounds and infuses character and narrative, blending description and thought.

The city multiplies in multicultural and refracted ways beyond the modernist novel. Take Italo Calvino's 1972 *Invisible Cities*, wherein a mythic Marco Polo describes cities to the Emperor Kublai Khan at the twilight of the Mongolian Empire. Polo evokes patterns of traffic and memory, exotic marketplaces, parades and caravans, demolitions and constructions, each city's resemblances to other cities. He explores the city's personal revelations for the traveller:

> Arriving at each new city, the traveler finds again a past of his that he did not know he had: the foreignness of what you no longer are or no longer possess lies in wait for you in foreign, unpossessed places.[7]

The cities Marco Polo describes, at first, are ancient or medieval, though later vignettes have distinctly modern and even futuristic sci-fi features. The multiplicity of Calvino's postmodernist structure reflects simultaneously on possible worlds, social spaces, and the ways travellers encounter, internalize, or self-reflect through them.

Many of Calvino's cities are impossibly utopian or dystopian, Platonic in their vivid conceptual performance of abstraction. One city constantly constructs itself but in so doing only constructs more and more cranes and scaffolds. 'If you ask, "Why is Thekla's construction taking such a long time?" the inhabitants continue hoisting sacks, lowering leaded strings, moving long brushes up and down, as they answer, "So that its destruction cannot begin."' What plan underlies this continuous remaking? 'Work stops at sunset. Darkness falls over the building site. The sky is filled with stars. "There is the blueprint," they say.'[8] Another city's public square regularly reassigns social roles and occupations; still another's entire architecture is suspended between two mountain peaks above a chasm. Some cities suggest the way travels intersect with ageing and memories of earlier visits. Isidora, revisited, matches the city of the ageing traveller's

> dreams: with one difference. The dreamed-of city contained him as a young man; he arrives at Isidora in his old age. In the square there is the wall where the old men sit and watch the young go by; he is seated in a row with them. Desires are already memories.[9]

Other cities stage the ways meanings overlay streets, like Tamara:

> You penetrate it along streets thick with signboards jutting from the walls. The eye does not see things but images of things that mean other things: pincers

point out the tooth-drawer's house; a tankard, the tavern; halberds, the barracks; scales, the grocer's.[10]

Even the merchandise of Tamara exists in an unreal semiotic web of desire and identity expression:

> the embroidered headband stands for elegance; the guided palanquin, power; the volumes of Averroes, learning; the ankle bracelet, voluptuousness. Your gaze scans the streets as if they were written pages: the city says everything you must think, makes you repeat her discourse, and while you believe you are visiting Tamara you are only recording the names with which she defines herself and all her parts.[11]

To travel to the city is to read it—and to write it. Much as signs and associations overlay architecture and objects for sale, cities invite imaginative stories interpolated into the lives of others, casting real people with their own separate existences into private fantasies. In Chloe, where the people 'are all strangers,' residents 'imagine a thousand things about one another; meetings which could take place between them, conversations, surprises, caresses, bites. But no one greets anyone; eyes lock for a second, then dart away, seeking other eyes, never stopping.'[12] Sometimes a city is different depending on the direction of arrival: one city if by sea, another if by desert. Or one for the traveller who looks up to the eaves; another who walks head down, observing only gutters and refuse. Or it is one city for travellers 'who pass it without entering' and 'another for those who are trapped by it and never leave.'[13] There is a city whose underworld recreates the city above so the dead will find the afterlife familiar and a city that throws all its objects away after a single use. And so on. Each city shows us an aspect of every city: the way cities construct themselves or distribute social relations or burn through history.

The Great Khan knows his cities only the way imperial power does: through military strategy, brute force, political maps. He does not know them through intimate, vulnerable encounters at the street level. Polo knows these cities instead as the traveller, which is another way of saying as the spectator (or, inverted, the actor): the one who sees and carries the city through poetic impressions, one who shares anecdotes that can only be performed, souvenirs that might only be valuable to the foreigner or Benjamin's rag-picker. When Khan asks Polo why he never mentions his native Venice, Polo insists that he has been all along: 'Every time I describe a city I am saying something about Venice.'[14] Polo never saw Venice so deeply, was never so profoundly Venetian, as when he travelled to all these foreign cities, as when he performed them for the Mongol emperor Khan. (At the same time, those cities may be no more than refractions of Venice through the prism of memory, desire, and dystopian visions of the city's future as it gradually sinks into the sea.) Polo also engages in a deeply imaginative anthropology with regard to the cities he experiences as a traveller, with some recognition of his own biased role

22 Writing (on) the city

as the Venetian ethnographer, attending to details and obscure traces, drawing from this rag-picker research to perform for Khan.

Cities contain their own pasts, 'like the lines of a hand, written in the corners of the streets, the gratings of the windows, the banisters of the steps, the antennae of the lightning rods.'[15] These remnants witness to memories that remain obscure to most long-time residents, never mind foreigners. Cities' memories may require the artist, the traveller, to draw out their memories—which can only happen through subjective readings, imaginings, rememberings, retellings. The subtle explorer pays attention to small traces of public memory usually neglected, divining their patterns through suggestive descriptions. But the sensory reality of these cities arises somewhere liminal, between the performer and spectator.

In *Invisible Cities*, the first few meetings between the traveller and emperor involve communication through souvenirs and leaps, cries and gestures, bridging the language gap with spontaneous acts that become symbolic descriptions. The Great Khan, listening in the fragrant evening breeze of a garden, interpolates his own images into the space between Polo's words and gestures. The miniature worlds constructed through fragments, objects, and anecdotes animate invisible cities, remembered cities, impossible cities. There are remembered cities the traveller performs and imagined cities the emperor sees as he embarks on interior journeys, interpreting with an eye to the mythic and prophetic. Then there are the cities the reader imagines by interpreting Calvino's often allusive, illusive prose. The act of reading this novel necessarily involves readers' memories of the city streets they have traversed or imagined before, including through other novels, travel shows, and films. Since the arrangement of the book rewards non-linear excursions between short vignettes that depict separate cities, the act of reading resembles the very act of travel that underlies Marco Polo's source material. Memories and choices scaffold virtual travel, structuring both the familiar city and its opposite: the fantastical, utopian (or dystopian) city that stretches known urban experiences into exemplary visions. By imagining urban spaces, these fellow travellers (explorer, emperor, reader, writer) unspool the kinds of riddles cities ask of travellers, 'like Thebes through the mouth of the Sphinx.'[16] They meditate on enigmas about themselves, dwelling and travel, empire and myth, about what it means to be a subject in the context of history. Together they perform the imaginative act of making the invisible city visible.

Notes

1 Jeremy Tambling, *The Palgrave Handbook of Literature and the City* (Palgrave, 2016), 8.
2 Alain de Botton, *The Art of Travel* (Vintage, 2008). 183.
3 James Joyce, *Ulysses* (Shakespeare, 1928), 164.
4 Teju Cole, *Open City* (Random House, 2012).
5 Tambling, *Palgrave Handbook*, 2.
6 Ibid., 36.
7 Italo Calvino, *Invisible Cities*, trans. William Weaver (Harcourt Brace Jovanovich, 1974), 28–9.

8 Ibid., 115.
9 Ibid., 8.
10 Ibid., 13.
11 Ibid., 14.
12 Ibid., 51.
13 Ibid., 113.
14 Ibid., 86.
15 Ibid., 10–11.
16 Ibid., 44.

3
PERFORMING (IN) THE CITY

Marco Polo begins to lose his communicative magic once he grows more fluent in the Levantine languages at the court of the Mongolian Empire. For Kublai Khan, as the traveller's words grow clearer and begin to lose ambiguity, his descriptions begin to lose also their original, spontaneous, embodied presence borne of the necessity to communicate outside language. Polo's gestures and spontaneous acts of imaginative connection prove more potent stimuli to Khan's urban imagination than words alone.

Most of the following pages weave my memories of travelling through cities in and out of descriptions of Teatro Potlach's long-term site-specific theatre project inspired by and named after Calvino's *Invisible Cities*. While Calvino's text haunts both the form and content of this book, I am particularly interested in exploring Teatro Potlach's event inspired by those words and taken into the streets, into embodied, immersive, site-specific performance. Perhaps ironically, the central concern of this book is to investigate the city's artistic significance beyond what books can point to. If literature, like Calvino's novel, helps readers see interwoven networks of meaning, performance, like Teatro Potlach's *Invisible Cities* and Polo's descriptions, touches the traveller's encounter with the city's deepest rhythms.

Many writers who have thought seriously about the aesthetic nature of urban life, from Freud to Calvino and Solnit, depict cities textually, through metaphors of reading or writing, as palimpsests and so on. But performance underlies cities' myths, political geographies, and daily rhythms. The city unfolds in ways that texts alone can account for no more than a static two-dimensional map can account for a century in the life of a metropolis—even if, as in Borges' fable, it is enlarged to a life-size topography of the territory, laid point-for-point on top of the landscape it represents. Even an infinitely detailed static map would lack the temporal and embodied horizons so foundational to urban experience. As D.J. Hopkins, Shelley Orr, and Kim Solga note in their essay collection *Performance and the City*, performance is text's 'precursor, the long-disavowed engine of much of the city's cultural power.'[1] For example, Graeme Miller's 2003 sound installation *Linked* relied quite a lot on words but depended most fundamentally for its absent presence on the live disappearing act of performance. The piece was designed to be heard from radio transmitters along the margins of the M11 Link Road in the East End of London—these transmitters picked up a collection of stories of the displaced, uprooted former residents whose houses were demolished to make way for the road. Miller framed the work with reference to de Certeau's essay 'Walking in the City.' The performance is, Miller suggested, an opportunity to 'rewrite' the urban narrative. But Solga (et al) writes of experiencing *Linked* that she did not 'feel much like writing' afterwards, that the piece:

> rather requires a different way of thinking about both the city and its stories: it requires me to traverse the line between privacy and publicity; it requires the attention of an actor (where is the next transmitter; where is my next cue?), the creative generosity of an audience member (how do I connect to, feel for, this disembodied voice?), and an affective, whole-body immersion in the spaces of its words. People, birds, cars; take-away curries and diesel exhaust; wrong turns, sore ankles, and relived discoveries: I'm not just piecing together a story. I'm taking part in the rehearsal of a community, its rebuilding via its collective restaging.[2]

In this sense, performance is the very stuff of the city, and therefore offers a concrete way to reveal or intervene in a city's routes. As Jen Harvie notes in *Theatre and the City*, theatre particularly marks performance into a kind of urban synecdoche. A miniature concentration of the city's dynamic complexity, theatre is 'symptomatic of urban processes, demonstrating the structures, social power dynamics, politics and economies also at work more broadly throughout the city.'[3] A microcosm and magnifier, the theatre often becomes the place where the city's invisible forces are made concrete and visible. For Harvie, this microcosmic relationship between theatre and city centres on the political. Economic and other power relations play out in ways that connect the *polis* to its civically situated theatres, from the naming of theatre districts to site-specific interventions in commercial or public spaces.

The interaction between cities and performance has provoked top performance studies theorists and artists to think deeply about the nature of everyday life and specifically dimensions of urban subjectivity. Nicolas Whybrow's edited volume of essays *Performing Cities* includes Sue-Ellen Case on the postmodern sprawl of Los Angeles, Matthew Ghoulish on Chicago's demolition of seven significant buildings, Mike Pearson and Heike Roms on Cardiff's performance pasts, Paul Rae's interrogation of the city/state performed by Singapore, Freddie Rokem's consideration of religious and political performance in Jerusalem, María Estrada-Fuentes analysing Bogotá's traumatic memories of urban bombing, David Williams thinking through Pina Bausch's *Palermo Palermo*, and so on. As Whybrow notes, cities appeal to performance theorists in two crucial ways: firstly, 'we may view the city as a whole, or indeed a particular aspect of it, as a performing entity or performance in its own right'; cultural behaviours, architectural mise en scènes, and socio-economic contexts activate the city's possibilities and frame performative identities. This inherently performative dimension of urban life also interacts with explicit forms of cultural production, such as site-specific artworks 'that address a particular aspect of the city or effectively perform the city into a kind of being—however temporary— via their particular forms of engagement with or intervention in urban space.'[4] Site-specific performances—including pieces created by Fiona Templeton, Graeme Miller, Blast Theory, Wrights & Sites, Brith Gof, Rimini Protokoll, Spell#7, and Teatro Potlach—often engage the city as both subject and stage; they can unveil a city's invisible forces in particularly concrete and dynamic ways. As Jane Collins notes, site-specific performance often has 'no fixed stage edge; the line between the fictional space and the real is fluid and unstable.'[5] This fluidity often forces spectator-travellers to encounter the city through an intimate and physical dialogue with its spaces, blending performers, spectators, architecture, and passers-by.

The Welsh artist Mike Pearson, along with the group he has long worked with, Brith Gof, has created performances that involve spectators encountering urban environments in Cardiff through direct and layered interactions with sites haunted by what they have been, by what has transpired—even when only obscurely perceptible traces remain. Pearson sees site-specific performances as 'conceived for, mounted within and conditioned by the particulars of found spaces, existing social situations or locations, both used and disused: sites of work, play and worship: cattle-market, chapel, factory, cathedral, railway station.'[6] The histories and everyday engagements with these spaces interact with the performances that arise from them, creating an intricate interplay between past and present, between the lived city and the remembered (or forgotten) city. From Fiona Templeton's *YOU—The City*, a journey for one spectator at a time through lower Manhattan, to Blast Theory's *Rider Spoke*, a performance piece/interactive game for cyclists near the Barbican in London, site-specific performances often make spectators pay special attention to their presence as co-creators of urban experience who encounter phenomena that may resist their stories.

One of the most influential performances to engage the city as both performance and text, Forced Entertainment's *Nights in this City* put spectators on a bus tour through Sheffield—and, in an iteration two years later, Rotterdam. Over the course of a drive through this city, the tour guide Alan (visibly and audibly drunk) narrated local, often inappropriately personal stories while pointing out warehouses and street corners. Members of Forced Entertainment, like Benjamin's rag-picker, researched for the piece by collecting discarded scraps of writing found on the street and conducting interviews with locals about where in Sheffield one might best bury a body or bid farewell to a lover. The inebriated guide Alan was generally unreliable on facts. He described on Love Street 'the place where they're thinking of building a new McDonald's' and followed it with dubious local history: 'All the streets round here got named after famous football hooligans from history and all the buildings got named after ghosts and cleaning products and convicted kerb crawlers.' He warned the spectators 'that geography's never exactly been my strong suit.'[7] The tour was unsteady, marking a blurry separation between urban travel and the traveller's mental stories that unfold along the journey. The performance invited an exchange between stories spectator-travellers projected onto the city and the city's performance of itself, as the director Tim Etchells put it:

> What a strange project this is, with its audience and performers inside a bus slipping through the centre of its cities and out of control—off the beaten track, playing always to the differences between on-route and off-route, centre and periphery, with versions of truth both legitimate and illegitimate. In the end perhaps it is simply a guided tour of the unremarkable, of the banal made special. The text we've created—pointing out buildings, street corners, carparks, patches of wasteground—is always overlaid with other texts—with the whispered or even shouted texts of other passengers ('*That's where I used to work… That's the place where…*') and the silent text of actions created by those living and working in the city as the bus moves through it. Sometimes it seems as if all we have to do is gesture to the windows and ask people to look.[8]

Through that gesture that beckons them to look, the passengers can see both their projections of stories and the city's resistance to being written upon. Etchells notes how 'where we talk of magic there is simply an ugly dual carriageway.'[9] *Nights in this City* draws out the layered complexity of urban travel. It questions travellers' perceptions and touristic curations but also urban subjectivity itself, the way subjects construct themselves and each other through the intricate textures, memories, myth-making, and patterns of meaning that unfold through the city.

Nights in this City performs not only the dialogue between different stories but also the displacement and instability lurking in any attempt to connect to the city. Nick Kaye touches on this dynamic in *Site-Specific Art*, noting that the 'dream-like journey through Sheffield's backstreets and housing estates' complicates the need to connect through 'incongruous representations of the city's spectacles.'[10] The 'journey evokes an inability to rest in the places toward which the audience's attention is directed' and so 'articulates a curious displacement from a site whose particularities cannot be easily or appropriately named.'[11] While amplified in *Nights in this City*, displacement and the inability to fix experience with stable names are inherent to modern travel's mediations by technology (microphone, bus, traffic signs). In its engagement with the city of Sheffield, including the private homes of its poor citizens, Forced Entertainment intertwined the apparatus of theatre somewhat uncomfortably with that of tourism, using these two modes of mediating urban space to question each other. As Fiona Wilkie notes in *Performance, Transport and Mobility*, this journey 'invokes the tourist technologies of its vehicle—the guide's microphone; the windows framing a moving scene; the tactics for ascribing meaning to a shared itinerary—at the same time as it undermines the reliability of these technologies.'[12] Like other site-specific, transportation-based theatre, especially in the U.K. since the late 1990s, *Nights in this City* draws attention to the theatrical dynamics always at play as we move through cities and suggests ways these technologies can distort even as they mediate travellers' pictures of the world.

Related pieces aboard vehicles have more pointedly explored the politics of public and private spaces as seen from passenger seats. For instance, Anna Pharoah's curated series of performance installations called *Five-Second Theatre* (2005) self-consciously theatricalized domestic views seen from a passing train in Hull. Actors performed scenes in windows of private homes, for example eating spaghetti or engaging in other domestic tasks. By 'apparently reinforcing the position of train passengers as voyeurs,' Wilkie suggests, these performances reflect the separation and othering of that position as rooted in the technological power—and politics—of speed.[13] Insofar as 'ocular domination' derives from a technologically or velocity-based power differential, it is often accompanied by a numbing effect that reduces traversed city views to just that: moving pictures, spectacles for the traveller's consumption rather than spaces for meaningful encounters. Performances that involve travelling as their very substance may not only reveal hidden aspects of urban life but even attempt to resist its coercive, anesthetizing tendencies. As Wilkie shows, walking performances can particularly open the spectator to modes of engagement and intimacy missing in bus, car, or train rides.

Performance artists from Tehching Hsieh and William Pope.L to the members of Rimini Protokoll have often explored urban performances as ways to highlight labour that invisibly underlies cities. In her 'Maintenance Art,' Mierle Laderman Ukeles draws attention to the work of janitors, sanitation workers, and caretakers, people whose vital energetic commitments keep cities going beneath the streets, behind the scenes, inside the homes—and often without just compensation. Ukeles frames these conventionally invisible labours as performances by executing them with spectators in mind, or signalling through photographic documentation labourers in their work; these tasks become then not only actions oriented towards maintaining urban order but events oriented towards the viewing public who might otherwise take them for granted. In this way, Ukeles also shows how performance can help people see the invisible city. Like the rag-picker described by Benjamin, certain performance artists have explored the alleyways behind the storefronts and theatres to expose the city's guts, its digestive processes and sources of energy, its ways of maintaining life.

In revealing the invisible city, these artists may perform a more aesthetically serious version of what the engaged traveller often does. The traveller can follow impulses and interests to peer into the contradictions or to go behind the scenes of cities. An inverse of the traveller-as-flâneur, the traveller-as-rag-picker looks closely at seemingly insignificant details, trying to let the textures and secrets of a place speak. But of course travellers by no means necessarily or automatically see cities more deeply than residents do. Tourists, often notoriously, see little beyond superficial artifice—often in ways they try to overcome in ever more urgent quests for authenticity. This authenticity is paradoxically opposed to and sustained by the theatricality of tourism. Even travellers bent on breaking away from stereotypical tourist behaviour may find themselves ignoring most of a foreign city by moving between spots described by a beloved writer or introduced by local contacts. As Solnit notes in *A Book of Migrations*, tourism 'theatricalizes cities' by exaggerating their cultural peculiarities and making them legible to travellers, who reward such distortions financially and in turn behave like spectators when they visit castles and pubs. For cities whose architecture and customs morph to accommodate tourists, this theatrical dimension can be playfully theatrical but destructive to authenticity: Solnit compares tourism's effects to the waves of invasions by Vikings and the English that have left their mark, often violently, on Dublin—just as war and colonialism have ravaged and rebuilt so many of the cities people travel to see, from Mexico City to Cape Town.

Insofar as tourists enter the economic, political, and cultural activities of a city, they shape its appearance in theatrical ways. They complicate the city's dynamics between visible and invisible cultures. Cities popular to tourists can become curated versions of themselves that show off pleasant or significant aspects while hiding the banal or shameful. Dean MacCannell analyses the visible and invisible in cities from a sociological perspective, adapting Erving Goffman's structural division between 'front' and 'back' regions to understand tourism. The 'front is the meeting place of hosts and guests or customers and service persons,' MacCannell writes, 'and the back is the place where members of the home team retire between performances to relax and to prepare. Examples of back regions are kitchens, boiler rooms, executive washrooms, and examples of front regions are reception offices and parlors.'[14] The theatricality of the city's visible texture relies on an invisible backstage space that hides and protects, facilitating rest, costume changes, and moments of privacy. This dynamic resembles something theatre artists and theorists know well: the scene is undergirded by the unseen, the obscene. Off-stage actions or backstage space, as Andrew Sofer puts it, act like 'dark matter' that remains invisible but exerts force on the visible.[15]

Travellers with enough means and experience often grow restless, refusing to be satisfied with postcard landmarks or obviously curated shopfronts. Their touristic desire is arguably not so different than Forced Entertainment's or Ukeles' aesthetic impulses to expose in cities what others miss. Many want to penetrate the spectacle, to go beneath even what locals see. Catering to a hunger for 'authenticity,' the backstage tour (of a city's grand opera, say, or brewery) seems to promise something real and hidden, revealing operations that most never see. So, MacCannell notes, the

> tour is characterized by social organization designed to reveal inner workings of the place; on tour, outsiders are allowed further in than regular patrons; children are permitted to enter bank vaults to see a million dollars, allowed to touch cows' udders, etc. At the same time, there is a staged quality to the proceedings that lends to them an aura of superficiality.[16]

The very drive for the authentic invisible beneath the veil of culture renders even 'invisible' production and daily life theatrical, leaving no definite boundary between onstage and off. The invisible recedes further into the shadows as soon as you try to throw a spotlight on it, undermining any stable site of the 'authentic' city.

Unlike a backstage tour that promises authentic access but delivers further superficiality, the sort of performance I am highlighting in the pages that follow seems to promise a form of artifice (theatre) but then attempts to unveil through that artifice real ghosts the city otherwise hides. In this sense, contemporary site-specific performance joins a deep and ancient tradition in theatre. The city's complex intertwining of memory and desire, projection and identity, happens both onstage and off, and has probably been happening as long as there has been theatre: the City Dionysia in Ancient Athens staged plays on the south slope of the Acropolis; medieval mystery cycles moved through the streets of York and Oberammergau; Moros y Cristianos pageants commemorated Spanish Reconquista battles throughout Inquisition-era Madrid; the devotional Ramlila takes over whole cities like Varanasi; bourgeois commercial theatre dominates New York's Broadway and London's West End even as Happenings intervene in street life. Contemporary site-specific urban scenographers and performance artists such as Dorita Hannah and Shauna Janssen layer architecture and theatre into visions of invisible cities.

To travel through cities like a spectator is to attend to an essential theatrical dynamic. The point that interests me here—that the rest of this book pursues—is not merely that certain theatrical practices can unveil, express, or interact with invisible urban forces. The important point is that certain dynamics at the heart of cities (between the visibile and invisible, the everyday and extraordinary, self and world, past and present, nature and culture, public and private) are, at heart, theatrical: live, haunted by repetition, mediated by scenography, animated by performances and texts.

As I recall or reanimate cities, I am guided by Calvino's Marco Polo who so richly conveys cities he travelled through to Kublai Khan. But the act of imagining these cities is equally Khan's; such is the singular encounter of performance. When words fail, when objective description adds nothing to political maps or official histories, performance takes over: in fragments of experience, through anecdote, or embodied in an ostrich feather or seashell souvenir that symbolically invokes a city—while leaving 'space between the words' where the spectator can imagine, dwell for a bit, or wander away. In that spirit, the remembered cities that follow are only partial and highly subjective traces of my travels and my impressions of Potlach's *Invisible Cities*. Perhaps something in my experience stirs yours, prompting you to relive memories, to replay your travels in ways that remould past journeys into new pathways. Or maybe you will find here hidden alleyways you have never visited. Then maybe memories of your travels may spark a journey made of the cities you have seen, of what you might imagine, desire, or fear in a city.

Notes

1 Kim Solga, Shelly Orr, and D.J. Hopkins, eds. *Performance and the City* (Palgrave, 2009), 3.
2 Ibid.
3 Jen Harvie, *Theatre and the City* (Palgrave, 2009), 7.
4 Nicholas Whybrow, ed. *Performing Cities* (Palgrave, 2014), 2.
5 Jane Collins, 'Embodied Presence and Dislocated Spaces: Playing the Audience in *Ten Thousand Several Doors* in a Promenade, Site-Specific Performance of John Webster's *The Duchess of Malfi*,' *Performing Site-Specific Theatre*, Anna Birch and Joanne Tomkins eds. (Palgrave, 2012), 54.
6 Mike Pearson, *Site-Specific Performance* (Palgrave, 2010), 23.
7 Tim Etchells, quoted in Nick Kaye, *Site-Specific Art: Performance, Place and Documentation* (Routledge, 2013), 15.
8 Ibid., 22.
9 Ibid.
10 Kaye, *Site-Specific Art*, 9.
11 Ibid.
12 Fiona Wilkie, *Performance, Transport and Mobility: Making Passage* (Palgrave, 2014), 98.
13 Ibid., 59–60.
14 Dean MacCannell, *The Tourist: A New Theory of the Leisure Class* (University of California Press, 2013), 92.
15 Andrew Sofer, *Dark Matter: Invisibility in Drama, Theater, and Performance* (University of Michigan Press, 2013).
16 MacCannell, *The Tourist*, 98.

4

CITIES AND DREAMS
San Francisco

When I was a child I had a recurring dream about a city in the clouds. From a distance that made the city into a stage set, the buildings apparently floated, their shared base shrouded in fog. The invisibility of these foundations created an illusion that defied gravity. At some uncertain point, I found myself in a car crossing a boundary, a river Styx, or misty bay. Once within the city, my fellow passengers—my father and sister—and I suddenly reached a new point of view. The streets were so steep that driving uphill pressed our backs against the car seats like astronauts. My gaze pointed upward where barely visible pedestrians leaned against the hills, into their steps, clutching their coats close against the mist and the wind. Beyond and between them: radiant fog.

I most distinctly remember the moment this dream always tilted from wonder to terror. The car slowly arrived at the crest, pausing at the intersection. It lingered as if a roller coaster at the beginning of its first plunge. We levelled out and began to lean forward. Looking through the windows was like looking through those of a plane descending into a cloud. Then a patch of fog cleared in front of the windshield and we suddenly saw what lie below: a pile of hundreds of cars that had plummeted there before ours. The street was unfinished, but apparently no one could see until it was too late. I always woke up just before we fell.

At the age of eight or nine, my father took my little sister and me on vacation to San Francisco. We drove up the coast, stopping to collect clams on the beach. As the city emerged from the fog, I immediately recognized it from my dreams. And I knew I had to live there one day. For the better part of my twenties I did, in San Francisco's Noe Valley at the intersection of Jersey and Church. Through the curtained bay window in the apartment's only room, my girlfriend and I sat drinking coffee all day, watching the fog pour down thick between Twin Peaks. I drove her Toyota Echo down steep hills or rode the brilliantly scenic J-Church light rail, the windows a theatrical display of the city. I biked to the Caltrain, where I watched the repurposed warehouses of SoMa give way to the city's backstage: machine shops, junkyards, suburbs, the towns of the Peninsula and Silicon Valley. I explored neighbourhoods by bike and bus, watching them emerge from curtains of fog as if miniature theatres. I biked through the Mission looking at Mexican murals and communist coffee shops. I dragged myself up misty narrow streets at improbable angles through Bernal Heights, pausing where I could watch the whole city stretched below.

In her 'Atlas' of San Francisco, *Infinite City*, Rebecca Solnit notes how a ride on the 22 Fillmore bus makes it possible to see a cross section of the city. Passengers watch their neighbourhoods unspooled in a display of diversity and inequality.

> Fillmore Street runs through San Francisco's wealthiest neighborhood, Pacific Heights; drops into the gritty, African American Western Addition, known as the Fillmore District or just the Fillmore in its heyday; and then continues onward through the lower Haight, to end not far from upper Market Street and the Castro.[1]

Riders glimpse these neighbourhood's constituent pasts: 'The war between the states left its traces here, as did the Second World War, and the war on poverty, the war on drugs, the stale and ancient war that is racism, and various forms of freelance violence.' In the Haight, residue of the 1960s lingers, sometimes movingly in music and political action, though as you approach the McDonald's across the street from Golden Gate Park, you can see its legacy curdle into something rougher.

The Castro has staged self-consciously theatrical processions since the 1970s, leading the world's pride parades with boldly sexual and 'out' acts like the Sisters of Perpetual Indulgence. Aaron Surin aligns the flourishing lives of butterflies and LGBTQ+ culture in a city that becomes a radiant ecosystem once a year:

> Out of the old bars into the raging streets, out of the private societies into City Hall, out of the psych wards and into the wards of voting booths, from bitter dark rooms to ecstatic back rooms, from paddy wagon to parade... Didn't the city itself change shape, burst through, take wing, blaze into color, catch fire and light?[2]

The politics of this ecosystem not only grew towards liberation in San Francisco; San Francisco led cities around the world to bring queer life into public, as part of the polis. It makes sense that a public 'coming out' party invoked theatrical traces from festivals in other cities—Carnival in Rio, Mardi Gras in New Orleans. Theatrical festivals are at the heart of the city's public expressions and performative freedom. The stage itself in San Francisco has been the site of emancipatory acts like Kushner's 'Gay Fantasia on National Themes' *Angels in America*; San Francisco's performances have reimagined gender and sexuality through subversion and mythic speculation.

I returned to San Francisco in 2016 to help spread the dead's ashes with old friends. Carl Weber had died: an influential director, a beloved teacher (including to Kushner) who had taught at NYU and Stanford after a career at the Berliner Ensemble, a man who had worked directly under Brecht and later translated many Heiner Müller plays. After a long and productive career, his former students gathered to say goodbye. The evening by the ocean was moving, and the sense of returning to this city to see these old friends reminded me how central San Francisco had been not only to shaping culture and history but also the particular imaginations of people I'd known and loved and worked with. It had been almost a decade since I had seen the place. Travelling once-familiar streets again the morning after the memorial, I was struck by the dark side of the city's theatrical appeal. Hardware stores had given way to lotion boutiques. An old diner named Herb's on 24th Street became a faux-chrome travesty called Toast. Brunch plagued every corner. Families of Mexican and Venezuelan heritage that had been here for generations were priced out of the Mission in favour of Google, Apple, Twitter, and Facebook employees. Increasingly the city seemed transformed into a playground for the super-rich. Its colours and shapes, its visual worlds, had always leaned into visual flourishes, from the Painted Ladies to the Golden Gate Bridge. But now this city—once so boldly countercultural, so challenging to the establishment—has curated its neighbourhoods into gauche spectacle sold to hungry eyes. How can cities encourage theatrical visions of liberation flourish without becoming devoured by them?

Notes

1 Rebecca Solnit, *Infinite City: A San Francisco Atlas* (University of California Press, 2010), 68.
2 Aaron Surin, *Infinite City*, 49.

5
CITIES AND MEMORY
Fara in Sabina

The traveller enters Fara in Sabina through an arch in its medieval city wall. The frame of this arch, along with the upward incline of the narrow cobblestone street, suggests a theatrical set. But then you pass through. You enter the proscenium. You cross the mysterious threshold. The houses are high, some four floors, and close together. The balconies and alleyways and stairs and unrepaired ruins of homes come together like a strange dream, like an M.C. Escher drawing or forgotten fairy tale. Walking through the city, you encounter the alleyway of the cats, the stairway to nowhere, the bakery beneath the bell tower. You go up, always up, and you find the theatre perched at the top of the hill, the top of the city: Teatro Potlach, the group that has performed here for nearly half a century.

Fara in Sabina is medieval in the way only an Italian hilltop village can be. Its essence, its invisible structuring principle, is not Roman but Lombard. Amidst the collapse of the Empire, its current form arose from the imaginations and labour of Germanic and Frankish 'barbarians' who descended from the north, where far beyond the Alps and even the Rhine they had forged tribes of the forests: worlds beyond the reach of Rome. Amidst the fertile valleys that once grew olives for senators and centurions this village rose like a citadel, one whose narrow alleyways connect stone houses and hide secret gardens. You can still see traces of old ways in stone steps worn from millions of feet stepping on just the same spot. You can hear the old notes in the songs mothers sing at dawn. You can feel the angles of a labyrinthine sensibility. But you can see too the power of Rome: the Orsini wealth in the massive palace, the church in the piazza built on the remains of an altar to some obsolete god, the dialect that overlays every personal greeting.

The village's deep past is much older. Not only is it much older than these medieval origins, it's much older than the Roman Empire. The Sabine people have been cultivating these hills for millennia, preserving food, transporting salt, growing olives. Their DNA lives on, invisibly, in the first Romans, who mythically raped the

Sabine women back from these hills to breed the citizens of the first city: the basis for the kingdom and republic and empire to follow.

★★★

A tale of two Francescos:
We went early on a Thursday. Francesco Bellini, the warm, studious, always-smoking 91-year-old man whose house I am staying in—as much museum as house, stuffed, as it is, with relics, maps, souvenirs, pieces of Fara in Sabina history—invited me yesterday to go with him to see his land. At least that's what I had gathered, and it proved true. We communicate a lot but share few words. He is one of the only people in this town who speaks less English than I speak Italian. Anyway, he invited me, and I went. I could communicate that I accepted his invitation, and that, on the drive, the countryside was beautiful, the vistas, the panoramic views, but I could not convey that I had been here yesterday. Yesterday with another Francesco in fact.

This other Francesco—much younger, 38, and a kind of Casanova with soul patch and shoulder length curls—has a farm too, and very near the land of Francesco the Elder. Francesco the Younger drove me past his agritourism farm to see the biggest olive tree in Europe, and, at over 2400 years, one of the oldest. Along the way we walked through mountain trails to find old food storage places carved out of the rock, he taught me about the pre-Roman Sabine people, and then he showed me how these old places are buried under ancient and medieval and modern architecture or overgrown by vines. On the drive back he asked me why we study the past. Before I could answer he told me that the prehistoric Sabine people collected flowers—why? He told me it was because the past always grows the future as a gift, where pollination expands its seeds into new soil. He said the study of past civilizations was not about nostalgia or golden ages or even preservation, but that it should be directed towards a future unity, when all people will participate in a new economy of gifts, where we will no longer exchange in cold calculated ways, efficiently measuring value through abstractions and mathematical precision, where we will no longer have to guard surpluses and thus will no longer need war or economic struggle. We should just become like the sun, he said: live out, give out, become again the promise of what once was, back in archaic pre-Sabine roots, but now riding on the rivers of international cooperation between far-flung tribes.

Francesco the Elder told me no such things, or maybe he did and I couldn't understand his Italian. But he did show me his land, where he too grows olives, where his ancestors have for generations. He fed his birds and horses, he showed me his trees. They were old and had names that I have forgotten. I have been staying in Francesco the Elder's house these past weeks, a house like a museum. It contains centuries of memory, and only on this trip to the country could I start to piece together the source of his mental and material being. He lives in a house and tends the land where his father Stefano, and grandfather Francesco, and great-grandfather Stefano, and great-great grandfather Francesco, and so on, also lived and tended and dwelled. In his land are old trees whose olives were turned into oil for the villages in these hills. Francesco's house is saturated with centuries of tobacco smoke and totems to times gone by: fragments of statuary, old maps of Fara in Sabina, faded sepia photographs of generals decorated in shining medals. I began to try to form the words to ask what his father did during the war, then thought better of it.

This is a city, like any city, whose relationship to the countryside is fundamental but largely invisible. I can see the vast valleys below from the panoramic vistas on Francesco's balcony, but these do not show us how the bottles of oil come from these trees, how the trade in those olives once fed the economy that made this city possible, how the long droughts and then recent tragic freeze just before harvest time devastated farmers and the local economy.

To return to Fara in Sabina is to wind up roads through these olive trees, part of the invisible soil from which the city grows. Even its stones are from these hills. The agricultural and manual work that remains outside the city walls has furnished the city's food, all its wood, all its leatherwork and stonework minerals and architecture. Once atop the hill, you look down at the valleys below, the other hills, and see beyond to that great distant haze, where, on a clear day, with binoculars, you can see the dome of St. Peter's.

In the heart of this little city of 300 residents is a museum neither medieval nor classical but archaic: a building full of Sabine archaeology. Here the stone artefacts, there the recreated hill-forts of a civilization much overlaid. Here, long before the fathers of all Romans raped their mothers from the Sabine hills, life: a way of life, of being (in) a city, forgotten now; at the centre of modern Fara in Sabina but an invisible remainder. For millennia the hills have watched women carry water, men mill wheat, children invent worlds that superimpose the steep walkways. But the hills bear no witness, have no voice. It is all the traveller can do to detect some vague haunting.

Yet the city remembers. The dead far outnumber the living, and always will—our numbers swell daily, but theirs do too, and every gain of theirs is a loss of ours. They will always be ahead, so maybe the city should be theirs. The dead constitute the majority, though their representation in city council comes only by proxy, through efforts to preserve history. The steps they took; the houses they built; the customs they started and passed down; the wars they fought; the torments they suffered; the temples they consecrated; the bells they rang; the stones they chipped; the desire paths they wore into grass, then paved into official pathways; the wild capers they picked from the walls where they grew between stones; the clocks they carefully repaired; the books they wrote; the words they spoke; the songs they sung to their little young; the ideas they had, they shared, they feared, they celebrated; the knowledge they treasured; the flames they kept; the gardens they grew; the cellars they hid; the hearths they tended: all of this is invisible to those of us living. And yet the city has its memory. Just as we can never see beyond our place walking down the street, just as the city exceeds our vision in all its multiplicity in space, it expands beyond our temporal frameworks: the city is a being, or a ground of being, beyond the lifetimes of its little beings. If you listen closely, you can hear the city's memory. You can almost detect the ghostly presence of its ancient patron god.

When you go away it is hard to hold the city's reality in your mind. The same is true of fellow travellers from dozens of places around the world, arriving for the annual intercultural theatre festival, or any number of meditation and art retreats that rent summer rooms from the monastery. The residents stay beyond August, but Fara in Sabina is not the same city by winter. It is cold and windy and empty. It is what it always was: a small village in the province of Rieti. Each June, though, it arises atop the mountain, transformed for two weeks from a remote village into a magical, temporary city of lights and strange images, where residents and travellers from Tehran to Rio de Janeiro can do the weird, rich work of relating across cultures. The city wakes up from its hyperlocal slumber into a radical globalism, and yet its size and remoteness make it feel perennial, a Brigadoon.

6
INVISIBLE CITIES 1

Pino Di Buduo: In some way Invisible Cities *is a pilgrimage. The* percorso *[path] is to wash the spectator.*
Kyle Gillette: Like Dante's Purgatorio?
PDB: Yes. And so I begin with something more popular, more pleasurable and little by little I change the sensibility. So when you arrive to the end I can put something sublime.
KG: As in Fara Sabina 2016, Parvathy and the monastery. Tranquility.
PDB: You arrive higher, but if I put Parvathy at the beginning people wouldn't react. For this there is a dramaturgy, always, in Invisible Cities. *Because I can put this there, not here.*
KG: I think it's like, I'm a traveller with many suitcases. I walk and walk, and here I leave one and here I leave one and here I leave. I grow lighter and lighter. And I come to the top of the mountain and I see this: Parvathy. It's not that I gain. I lose.
PDB: Clean. Become clean. And when you become clean, I can put something the spectator can appreciate, can be inside, can stop and see, where she is singing.

On a warm evening at the beginning of July 2017, hundreds of spectators gathered in front of the Caffè Belvedere. Here near the top of a steep hill, just below the gates to the medieval village of Fara in Sabina in the province of Rieti, beer and gelato at sunset gradually gave way to espresso and digestivo at twilight. The spectators came from the surrounding villages of the Sabine hills and the valley below but also Rome, Berlin, Budapest—as far away as Tehran and Rio de Janeiro. They dressed casually, carried themselves (or their children) jovially. They watched a mismatched group of performers from different worlds assemble.

Daniela Regnoli, the co-founder of Teatro Potlach, incanted into a microphone. She spoke words she has uttered in dozens of cities and languages across Europe and the Americas, though tonight in Italian: 'Spectators, follow us; this voyage will take

FIGURE 6.1 Drawing by Beverly Morabito

you to the invisible cities hidden by the walls of houses and the weight of boredom.' She invited us to 'follow the path of sounds, walk alongside the images,' to 'see the apparitions of the seers and the splendor of the blessed, the market of passions and the suburb of the nomads.' Her text stressed spectators' role as travellers, not passive audience members; they were here to explore the city: its mysteries and nuances, its economies of desire.

Surrounding and behind Regnoli, actors from over a dozen countries wore costumes from diverse performance cultures. A Japanese Kamigata-mai master stood among masked commedia dell'arte actors and Persian T'azieh performers. Other figures hailed from contemporary Roman experimental theatres or comedy from Naples, or Tehran, Budapest, Rio de Janeiro…. No one seemed to be donning borrowed masks, either: these were committed practitioners working deeply in their respective traditions, many having done so for decades or generations. Parcans cast everyone in ghostly uplight. The wide beams threw mingled silhouettes up against the 15-metre-tall rock wall where wild capers grew between the cracks above the water fountain.

FIGURE 6.2 *Invisible Cities* by Teatro Potlach; photo by Sayna Ghaderi

Cameras and phones flashed everywhere. The atmosphere was charged with expectation. Not that spectacular weekend festivities feel out of place here. In the Sabine hills near Rome, if you go to a wedding or music festival it might well happen in Fara in Sabina, at the top of this high hill, in this tiny walled city whose architecture has changed little in the past half millennium. Even to show up on a random Saturday afternoon means to arrive in the midst of a city performing itself theatrically. Villages around here are becoming depopulated as the latest generation moves off to Rome, Milan, or London for professional careers, abandoning olive groves and local family businesses. The ones who remain supplement the town's economy by performing it for others. The 300 or so who live here maintain a shop, a bakery, a monastery that reward the tourist's gaze with performances of 'authentic' Sabine life. The very performance of that authenticity of course threatens it. Insofar as village-life clichés become photographable, quaint, they belie the vitality of the city as a site of the living, continuous with the dead. But this event feels different. Rather than threatening the village's complex and paradoxical life, *Invisible Cities* seems to magnify its paradoxes even as it apparently obscures or transforms city architecture through projections, lights, and cloths stretched over churches or through mysterious pathways. Rather than packaging daily practices as postcard visions, Potlach places these practices in foreign contexts that make them unfamiliar.

I had been here before. One year before, I stood in front of the same cafe. On that July night in 2016, Teatro Potlach, the theatre company that has called Fara in Sabina home since 1976, celebrated its 40th birthday and staged the 25th anniversary performance of its ongoing *Invisible Cities* project in the city where it all began. Under the direction of co-founder Pino Di Buduo, the group had staged dozens more *Invisible Cities* projects since the first one in 1992 all over the Europe and the Americas, as well as a few in Asia and the Middle East. The project began in Fara in Sabina but had not been performed here in 25 years. So the beginning of the journey just downhill from the archway, then up through the fabric tunnel, was a return.

I remember feeling an odd sense of recognition—odd in part because it extended beyond, before, my personal recollections—as the sun set beyond the hills and the summer heat dissipated off the cobblestones. It was unsettling to feel such significance when, otherwise, the texture of the evening was so typically Fara, so like what I've felt on many evenings here. The line of performers snaked up towards the gate in the medieval walls. The performers carried various levels of care in their steps. There were those in front who had spent their lives working with Teatro Potlach, some for the past four decades. They wore top hats or commedia masks or angel wings or flowing white dresses. They walked with purpose and precision. Just behind them, esteemed guests: from Japan clad in a Kimono and India in dreadlocks and long robes, from Iran wearing a tall feather in a gilded helmet. These performers were here for the past two weeks to teach morning workshops, perform theatre pieces in the evening, and collaborate on this *Invisible Cities* performance. Nino Rota's music immediately recognizable from Federico Fellini's film *8½* accompanied them, underscoring their journey cinematically.

Just behind them walked those who came from town: barbers, woodworkers, frame-painters, winemakers, folk dancers, choir singers, tai chi masters, antique restorers, children in dance classes. Also, schoolteachers and bureaucrats who sang in local choirs or played in local bands. They too would be performing, though for several of them that meant working the way they often do in their daily lives, behind closed doors. With a combination of active curation and passive openness to what others bring, Di Buduo interweaves performances of labour, traditional dancing, and music along the route such that spectators can see this work anew. These residents walked tentatively and less formally, not trained actors. It wasn't that they lacked skill and precision; it was that they hovered between everyday walking and the sort of care they might bring to a wedding or funeral. The concentrated intention of Teatro Potlach established a pathway that sanctified space. The townspeople whose work Potlach absorbed and intertwined with theirs walked along just behind the international collaborators as part of an intercultural mixture between the local and global.

Fara in Sabina is no Rome, though it is not far geographically—about an hour by car. Just over 50 kilometres and as many decades or even centuries away. If Rome is modern, cosmopolitan, Fara in Sabina is medieval, remote. If Rome is steeped in ruins and museums of the ancient empire, Fara in Sabina recalls a pre-Roman past, when archaic Sabine tribes traded salt with Etruscans beyond the hills, centuries before the Republic became an Empire. Rome's ruins are carefully preserved, lit beautifully by night, frozen in a tragic image of a fallen civilization (that can be glimpsed over cocktails from aperitivo bars across the street). Fara in Sabina has ruins too, but they are in the process of ruination still. A crumbling brick wall crumbles more each year I arrive. But it's not quite right to say these ruins go on crumbling out of sight either. People come here: locals from nearby villages, cyclists and motorcyclists, newly weds, Romans, city-dwellers looking for villages untouched by time, festival participants from cities all over the world, Austrian pilgrims who want to walk in the footsteps of San Francesco. The nostalgic, hyperlocal aura of the town meshes during Teatro Potlach's annual Festival Laboratorio Interculturale di Pratiche Teatrali (F.L.I.P.T.) with theatre practitioners from dozens of countries steeped in diverse traditions. In Rome this procession of artists from Brazil, India, the United States, Japan, Italy, Iran, Denmark, Hungary, and so on would shock less, merely the manifestation of multicultural cosmopolitanism the city has seen for centuries. Here in the little city of Fara, these cultures—intensified through performances staged nightly and workshops held daily—rest at night amongst nuns who continuously practice their order in a five-century-old convent and in the homes of residents whose ancestors have lived in the same houses for a dozen generations.

After the Teatro Potlach members, foreign guests, townspeople, and festival participants walked through the gate, spectators followed; the unbroken line seemed to emphasize continuity between performers and spectators, as well as between residents and travellers. In the beginning, we were all just pilgrims. We entered the gate into a long fabric tunnel that obscured the old walls as it led up the hill through the heart of the city. Like Dante's *Purgatorio*, it brought spectators through a liminal space that cleansed us of our everyday sediment as we walked up. The fabric

FIGURE 6.3 *Invisible Cities* by Teatro Potlach; photo by Sayna Ghaderi

tunnel hid buildings festival participants had walked for weeks, that the residents had walked for decades (and their ancestors: centuries, millennia). But long past midnight into the past three weeks, technicians and designers have been rigging ropes and cloth through the city walls' hooks and balconies. Tonight that labour was invisible, replaced by a fabric tunnel whipping in the evening breeze.

Along the way, performers peeled off, ducking into alcoves or doorways or harnessing themselves to repelling equipment along a path through town. They went ahead of the spectator-travellers and prepared the way. Regnoli, a mediating, shamanistic, Marco Polo presence between artists and spectators, led, held people back until the pathway was ready for exploration, invited them on again. Actors began, ahead of our sight, to execute their repeatable performances on a loop that would go on for hours. Spectators, eventually stretched more than a kilometre apart, walked past different kinds of performers embedded throughout the tunnel and in little stone alcoves; some of those we saw gathered in front of the cafe down below played music or recited poetry while others danced the Taranta or repeated everyday actions of washing or cooking in private homes. Near the arc in the medieval walls, we walked past two men singing 'Bye, Bye, Miss American Pie.' These two long-haired, bearded Pennsylvanians strummed a guitar, played a drum, drank from large Peroni bottles. People here in the past weeks could have seen a similar sight every night outside the bar, which inspired Di Buduo to incorporate it into the journey. Down through cellars and secret gardens, past books suspended from strings, musicians haunted corners and old churches. Clarinet and accordion music and opera songs drifted between miniature worlds. We filed past, some of us lingering to watch a scene a little longer, others skipping past to see the source of light around the corner. Our scenes changed with the pace of our steps, the direction of our gaze, with our attention and intention.

The tunnel passed the only hair salon in town, where the barber's deliberate actions took on special resonance. The tunnel also brought spectators past the restaurant L'Antica Bottega, where the fabric parted, like theatrical curtains, on the large window and all the diners inside. The waiters and diners were not part of the show. But of course they were. Their movements of serving, pouring, cutting, eating seemed a rich choreography, not just a particular group of people eating a meal but a quintessential Sabine restaurant scene framed by otherness, by strange lights and juxtaposed foreigners. Everything was inevitably drawn into the aesthetic journey, even the dog barking in the distance, whose voice later seemed to accompany a Kamigata-mai dance in a hidden courtyard by Keiin Yoshimura.

As I exited the long winding tunnel into a secret garden, it was as if I had arrived in another dimension hidden beneath the town's scenic surface. I walked past a man singing; he was in Persian T'azieh warrior costume. A woman in a wedding dress engaged him in a dance of anger and seduction in a secret garden I didn't even know was here. I went down into an alcove where an American man accompanied himself on the ukulele between words drawn from Henry David Thoreau spoken up close and in my face. I descended down narrow stairs into an unseasonably chilly wine cellar, where a woman dozed on a lawn chair in sunglasses, an open book

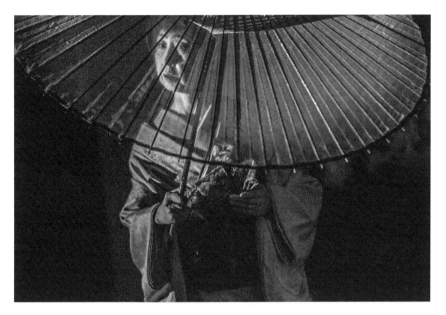

FIGURE 6.4 Keiin Yoshimura in *Invisible Cities* by Teatro Potlach; photo by Sayna Ghaderi

lying face down on her chest. But this vision had no place in such subterranean chill and darkness.

The course covered much of the town's historic centre, winding through convents and cellars and piazzas. Actors played scenes of longing or sorrow in the windows and doorways of narrow stone houses. Musicians were tucked behind walls that had deteriorated halfway to rubble. Rituals unfolded in private patterns, mourners weaving wreathes, lighting candles, chanting. Cellars and alcoves transformed into installations that mixed found objects with makeshift altars. Little bubbles of worlds recessed into the city breathed into it new vitality, mystery, depth. Woodworking, metallurgy, and pottery-making unfolded in dozens of tiny passageways; the products of this work accumulated in piles, transforming the scenography of the city in slow motion, through gradual sedimentation.

In 2017 the pathway began the same way, also through the tunnel of fabric, but then spilled spectators into a narrow alleyway to the right. The alleyway was just as narrow as the tunnel, but crowded with performances in the doorways and courtyards of private homes. Above, from balconies, a couple fought. They shouted at each other in a thick Neapolitan dialect between balconies of separate buildings. These actors were lit up by theatre lights jerry-rigged to lamp posts and window structures across the alleyway. They interacted in such a way that they seemed unconcerned that we were watching—except insofar as they made themselves audible, and pretended we were not here watching, taking videos on our phones. If it were not for these marks of performance, or if this were Naples, a city where private lives spill out of open windows, we travellers might have seen these people as rooted seamlessly in their context. Here, though, they were surrounded by opera singers and violinists and craftsmen and dancers and performance artists thickly interwoven with the fabric of this city.

Projections play a particularly potent role in Teatro Potlach's recent work, under the careful and relentless design of Vincenzo Sansone. As they cover and uncover architecture, I find myself attending less to the content of the projections than the contour of the buildings underneath. In the 2016 Fara in Sabina *Invisible Cities*, video projections from multiple projectors stitched together interacted with the stucco buildings that frame a piazza to invoke a tranquil Grecian sea, light blues and white moving along the stone and grout lines. In 2019, Nathalie Mentha danced through an astonishing theatre of cascades in the same spot. Projections of waterfalls intersected while fabrics blowing in the winds created a massive proscenium, whose curtains flowed with the rivers. She spoke texts from Goethe and Calvino, touching the mythic core of the Tiber in Rome, clad as a South American river goddess.

In 2017, past a red convertible with folk singers playing the ukulele, and the Beckettian head floating in the dark, up, up, up; past it all, I felt a moment of gentle transcendence. At the top of the hill is a monastery, haunting and imposing. I had been sleeping here every night, though only now did its walls breathe with new light. Before the gates, flanked by craftsmen, I paused to consider the pathway I had followed. Up, always up: already I had travelled through long fabric tunnels, through secret gardens, past installations and storytellers and opera singers embedded in private homes and church sanctuaries. On one side, as I walked towards the gates of the monastery, subtle shifts in patterns were projected onto walls far above, making

FIGURE 6.5 Zsofia Gulyas in *Invisible Cities* by Teatro Potlach; photo by Sayna Ghaderi

the old stones breathe. Above, a woman in angel wings seemed to float, suspended from a rope, dancing on the side of an old stone wall. Zsofia Gulyas, the angel figure, an acrobat from Hungary, was bathed in red light, lifting off and hovering mid-air before returning in slow motion to walk on the wall. She bent and shifted, flying to the music: a haunting Hindi or Sanskrit song coming from the other side underscored her every leap. Gulyas' angel dance has been repeated in some form in every *Invisible Cities* performance I have seen. In 2017, she was suspended high up a building at the main piazza, a spotlight circling her.

In 2018, Gulyas repelled off the side of the theatre's wall. In 2019, she was again at the gates of the monastery, haunted in my memory by her 2016 presence; she introduced Raphael's painting *The School of Athens* commissioned by Pope Julius II, readying travellers for the projections they would see and philosophy they would hear inside the monastery walls. At Trinity University in San Antonio, where as the Director of Theatre at Trinity University I invited Potlach to perform in 2015, Gulyas was suspended from the back wall of the theatre, drawing spectators' attention to the high fly system. Each instance of her presence manifested differently based on the architecture and surrounding performances. For example, in 2017, another aerial performer repelled opposite Gulyas from the bell tower, creating a sense of expansive space that invited spectators to look up, to appreciate the verticality of Fara in Sabina and the vast night sky above. In 2016, at the monastery, she seemed instead to sanctify the entrance to *Paradiso*. Opposite her that year, Parvathy Baul played a drum, turned fast in irregular, hypnotic circles, and sang. Her song felt saturated with love but also a yearning cry that would seem to come simultaneously from the core of her being and from outside herself, all around. She did not sing to us, the spectators, the travellers, as we ascended towards the gates of the monastery. Rather she sang in the opposite direction: to the valley below and beyond. Down from the hillside, to the other Sabine hills. Down to the villages and vineyards and olive groves, the tiny houses with lights twinkling. These houses throughout the valley felt folded into the stage, transcending distance. But I became aware too of our visual presence. Down there, looking up, villagers could see Fara in Sabina up above against the night sky, the lighted monastery rising above us. We were here like a beacon at the top of the high hill. Parvathy Baul sang across the wide below, across from the angel suspended, drifting, repelling off the crumbling convent wall.

Around the corner, craftsmen crafted, just outside the second set of gates. One man welded thin tubes, bending metal into outlines which, set between a floodlight and a muslin screen, projected immobile shadow puppets, something like the shadows of Plato's cave, but suspended, always on the verge of an action they would never take, a charge they would never begin. The figures were iconic, classical: horses and warriors and mythic heroes. The other side of the gate: a potter or woodcutter or sculptor, running a spinning spit, sparks and wood chips flying up, gathering at his feet. In through the gate, a tunnel with lighted plaques named previous *Invisible Cities*: Klagenfurt, Malta, Palermo, Londrina, Mazatlán.... I remember hearing, as I passed these reminders of a journey that has gone on longer than it seems possible, some opera, an aria. Was it Verdi? Puccini? The words and music warped as

I rounded the corner, masking what might be recorded, or live, or both. Mentha, the Swiss-born actress, moved gracefully with a long feather below a statue of San Antonio, as if dancing with him, though he witnessed silently, still as stone.

On past the other gates, headed towards the centre of town, an abandoned alcove of crumbling stones. A man sat smoking silently in the dark. His status in (or as) part of the work was dubious. In one sense, of course he was; everything was, just like the diners in the restaurant near the entrance. All people behaving, performing, or being in Fara in Sabina were gathered into perception by the rhythms and duration of these crafted journeys; all citizens and creatures participated in the unfolding of the work as an imagined city coterminous with the real city.

Another dog, this time an angry German shepherd, barked behind a gate as I ascended the hill. The fierce guttural sound seemed to attend the fallen Sansone, collapsed in red light after a monologue from Dante's *Inferno*. Cerberus: the monstrous three-headed watchdog of Hades—but here guarding what would become the gateway to a kind of exhausted transcendence. Like the dog near the fallen Sansone, and the great convent rising above the hill, like all the rocks and bell towers and rubble, and wind, and fellow travellers, the man smoking in the dark appeared (in this moment, and perhaps only for me and a few others): he felt significant, folded into the journey. This arrangement of the route through the streets, often saturated with juxtaposed performances, sometimes diffuse, meant nothing could be overlooked. Or rather, the inevitable fact of overlooking itself became unusually apparent: obviously no traveller could take much of the city in, but the juxtapositions between the theatrical and real amplified the intentional, fragmentary, contingent nature of the city's unfolding. To dismiss any detail as merely incidental (outside the sphere of art) was to miss the quality of attention the journey invited from us. We spectators—at times a mass, at times a great migration of little groups, at times lonely pilgrims lost in thought—could hardly help but attend to the journey in ways most often buried beneath habit and negligence.

Outside the gates of the monastery, a woman cooled herself with a rag and bucket of water on a crumbling stone outcrop. A tai chi master practiced in a fenced field, overgrown with weeds, surrounded by candles. A Roman theatre company performed Dante's *Inferno* below a ledge, where hardly any spectator could see. A woman from Puglia danced the Taranta to the beat of a drum, on loop near the rear entrance of the museum. With each repetition, the dance became more and more manic, finally exhausted, collapsed.

Within the museum were not just archaic Sabine artefacts but also a clown performing a comic bit in Farsi; I could not quite see him past the Etruscan pottery and reconstructed model hill-forts. But down below, through the windows, something else too: *bambini*! Children danced to the twenty-first-century American hip-hop and pop music in the piazza. Their routines could have come straight out of a dance class from the suburbs of Houston or Birmingham, mimicking boy bands and fly girls. The juxtaposition was startling, though it remained unarticulated, unframed by any discursive apparatus or explicit curation. Yet the idea was hard to miss. After a journey through Renaissance, Medieval, Classical, and pre-Classical

Invisible cities 1   **49**

FIGURE 6.6 Nathalie Mentha, Daniela Regnoli (et al.) in *Invisible Cities* by Teatro Potlach; photo by Sayna Ghaderi

allusions, spectator-travellers entered into the superficial exuberance of the young, the next generation who—unseen to all who have walked this earth, this hill—will (hopefully) go on living after we are all dead.

The path ended in the square by the old church, the travellers standing or sitting or watching or retreading steps, repeating the journey in reverse, or waiting casually for the procession of performers to arrive. As Di Buduo walked for the final time along the course, ending each discreet performance with a wave of his hands, all the performers fell into line, completing the journey as an inverted parade of spectators. And then at journey's end, outside the church and pre-Roman museum, outside the bakery, a great white sail of a cloth, much vaster than any sail I have seen, billowed from the bell tower.

The performers gathered, repeating the formation from down below by the Caffè Belvedere but now here, after a long journey, up above. Regnoli read the names of the artisans and dancers, the singers and actors, the tradesmen and women who composed the piece. (Down below, at the late night bar, we could hear roars of defeat; Germany had just beaten Italy in a football match.) The bell rang again; the performers made their way up to the theatre. Some spectators dispersed. Some retraced their steps. Some remained in the square, or drank late into the night.

I wandered up the walkways, and tried to remember moments that were already slipping into my memories of walking the same roads. I remembered bits I had seen, heard, felt, yet the impressions were scattered and impossible to pull together into a single, stable, coherent narrative. I replayed the journey in my mind, but I had not gathered images to hold onto. The city, as ordinarily experienced, became invisible, hidden beneath performances, cloths, projections. In its place, a normally invisible city emerged, a city made not only of Fara in Sabina's hidden pasts but also one haunted by other cities, one overlaid with cities travellers had brought with them. Customs and rituals bled and blended.

The next morning everything was gone. As they always do, the members of Teatro Potlach pulled down the cloths and projectors, the lights and structures, like thieves in the night. Walking along the path again on my way to breakfast, I saw the sun rise on walls that had been covered for weeks. I paid attention to aspects of the city that never popped out to me before. I watched the residents of Fara in Sabina wake up, walking their streets with open eyes, pausing at corners, seeming to remember something: a haunting image, some residue. Or maybe they were just relieved to see their beloved city back to normal, the exuberant festival participants on their way to the train station, the airport, away.

7
CITIES AND SPEED
Tokyo

The train flies across the city at night and suddenly you are 20 floors off the ground. Another train's path temporarily joins yours, less than 50 metres away, both of you soaring at slightly different velocities between neon skyscrapers. You are level for a moment with those other passengers packed shoulder to shoulder—their train barely moving relative to your speed even as the world whooshes past all of you. Those passengers are framed in glass portals that also reflect billboards above and behind you: a flash of a woman's giant holographic eyes, a neon parade of kanji, ads for yakitori and whiskey. For a moment, your relative velocities shift, such that you seem to be drifting backwards. A moment of vertigo. Yours then goes faster and you advance. Then your twin tilts down, disappearing between the buildings fanning along the boulevard, jutting 45 degrees away from your trajectory. You can only see the train's top, and then it snakes right, ducking into another network of pathways. Soon your visual field is swallowed by a tunnel, lights zipping by, leaving blurred traces on your retina.

The train pulls swiftly to a stop. The doors slide open. When you spill out and look back, efficiency specialists help push a new surge of passengers into the car before the doors slide closed. You look at the map; no help. Its jagged recursive complexity magnifies the unmappable vastness of this gridless city. You walk down the stairs into the street. Many udon shops sit only three stools at the narrow bar. Iced coffee machines line alleyways with no names and plastic tempura and ramen bowls advertise the real thing outside wooden doors. High female recorded voices repeat *konichiwa* outside sake bars and stores. A glass high-rise houses a Shinto shrine hologram that floats inside. Robed Buddhist nuns and suited businessmen pass teenagers with blue spiked hair sporting smartphones that make Silicon Valley teenagers seem Luddite. The Shinjuku neighbourhood envelopes the traveller into its thousands of signs clustered and refracted in tall alleyways, the ancient Edo interpenetrating the hypermodern Tokyo. The stone Buddha behind the sushi bar bears witness to a never-ending parade of bustle, ingenuity, desire.

Tokyo throbs with life, half techno-futurist, half old empire folded into intricate pagodas and origami birds. Nature appears in thousands of miniature theatres removed from the vast circuit board of city streets, in Zen gardens and bonsai trees and city parks where the craft of gardening is there not to tame flowers, trees, and stones, but to frame them, giving nature space to reveal its essence in singular details. Unlike the geometric gardens of Versailles, Tokyo offers asymmetry and organic wandering distilled by clearing away negative space. And just outside these little pockets of life, vast elaborate architecture and signs downtown flood the sky with light, a kaleidoscope of desires that blots out all simple expressions of natural growth. This is a city where performance expands perception, from the slow, controlled steps of the Noh or Kamigata-mai dancer to frantic parades of brightly coloured robots and the vivid, meditative visual worlds of the performance group Dumb Type. As with nature and architecture, Tokyo pulls the possibilities of performances in opposite directions until the fabric of the city bends.

The city performs far outside and between its theatres. In 1975, Senda Akihiko travelled through Tokyo with the eye of a theatre critic. He visited an empty store lined with broken clocks and toys, followed an arguing couple, and wondered: which objects were arranged for his viewing and which had he found the way they were? Which people were actors performing for him and which were just living their lives? He had to wonder because he was following a map created by Terayama Shuji, the artist responsible for creating many 'city dramas' wherein spectators visited dozens of sites without knowing whether they were curated, created, altered, or incidental. How, Terayama seems to ask, do spectators make meaning when theatre and the city intertwine?[1] This was the interesting question for Senda, who saw Terayama's work as meta on more levels than the theatrical. The question of how we determine meaning in theatre extends into the city, especially as we travel through it. What constitutes a frame within which specific appearances become meaningful? When does the bonsai go from an accidental outgrowth of organic life to a symbol of Japanese attitudes to nature? How do our desires drive and bend our perceptions, pulling us down crowded alleyways that make particular juxtapositions between a tempura shop and broken doll into a story? Where does the city end and the performance begin?

Note

1 Senda Akihiko, *The Voyage of Contemporary Japanese Theatre*, trans. John Thomas Rimer (University of Hawai'i Press, 1997).

8
CITIES AND SECRETS
Paris

You walk for eight hours through the Louvre, watching gawkers swirling around the *Winged Victory of Samothrace*; you try to see past a hundred amateur photographers holding their cameras high in front of the surprisingly tiny *Mona Lisa*. You wriggle your way through crowds in the Left Bank and across the river from Shakespeare and Company into the haunting gothic Notre Dame before heading to Le Centre Pompidou, the museum whose insides are out: pipes, ducts, scaffolding on the exterior walls, appropriate reflections of the city's experimental soul exhibited inside its galleries. You press through other tourists as you explore monuments, cafes, bookstores. Everything seems designed to be seen: as medieval, modern, or surging with life. If you arrive to these streets from the United States, or have been raised by Hollywood, your expectations may be primed by *An American in Paris*, giving you the secret hope that each quintessential view might give way to jubilant ballets backdropped by post-impressionist paintings. Paris may refuse or complicate its popular image by stealing your bag or stabbing you through your jacket, but Samuel Beckett got over the latter misfortune without it spoiling his cheery outlook on life, or Paris. He even met and forgave his attacker.

A certain aura of the city of letters, of philosophy, of revolution, is always here, lurking behind often disappointing reality like a faded postcard. In the eighteenth century, Paris was the epicentre of the French Revolution's Reign of Terror but also of Enlightenment thought. In the late-nineteenth century, it wore its world-leading fashion in display windows and elegant gardens. It was the place to be for certain modern artists and thinkers: expatriate painters like Van Gogh and Picasso; expatriate writers like Stein, Hemingway, and Beckett; interculturally minded stage directors like Ariane Mnouchkine and Peter Brook; thinkers from Sartre, de Beauvoir, and Merleau-Ponty to Lacan, Foucault, Derrida, Cixous, and Kristeva. Under Nazi occupation, the Resistance's hidden networks of message-relay made urban travel concretely subversive, and pregnant with urgent symbols—a landscape where you couldn't help but rethink the nature of language and social life. Paris streets were the epicentre of the May 1968 general strikes and university occupations, a revolutionary rejection of imperialist globalized capitalism and bourgeois spectacle that saw streets barricaded and buildings taken over, the work of government and commerce stalled. Paris has epitomized medieval scholasticism, aristocratic neoclassicism, and absolute monarchism, revolutionary liberation and violence, bourgeois *haute couture*, early communist experiments, expatriate bohemian culture, occupied fascism, and post-war postmodern intellectualism—often through theatrical urban gestures or in literal theatres.

The past century has internationalized the image-destination of Paris beyond Europe, while simultaneously drawing a large proletariat from North Africa and the Middle East that remains even more marginalized than the old French working class. These immigrants rarely appear centre stage for the tourist. If you are a tourist, you may however grow aware of the stories and perceptions of other travellers and residents, not (only) as characters in your drama but as spectators on their own journeys, experiencing their own changes of scene, their own investments in the people they watch. Tourists behold bridges and cathedrals, clutching cameras and looking up at gothic arches. Businesswomen and men navigate around wrought-iron planters, focused on getting to work or meetings. Waiters bustle between crowded cafe tables facing the boulevard, perhaps wrestling with Sartre's opinion of those who take their occupations too seriously. Seine artists and caricaturists paint or wait for customers, giving nearby streets the flavour of kitsch. Diners sip champagne cocktails at tables where they watch others walk by, looking into shop windows—where shoppers look at small trinkets and scarves, or each other, or back at observing passers-by. Their theatres intersect and intertwine, excluding or including each other in rolling tides of attention, through a rich variety of frames: art nouveau, wrought iron, often seductively curtained.

Paris is uniquely oriented towards people-watching, from cafe tables to park benches. Emile Zola urged the young director André Antoine simply to stage what one could see observing a morning at the food market Les Halles: the many classes and sorts of people intersecting, the foodstuffs and costumes far more interesting than the nineteenth-century stage's painfully artificial depictions of neoclassical tragedy, melodrama, and romanticism.[1] For some reason, the tenor of people-watching in Paris takes on darker shades than in some cities; every passer-by becomes a potential tragedy. Writers like Marguerite Duras who gravitate towards Paris can elevate bleakness to extraordinary levels of precision, concreteness, and elegance. Paris is a good place to feel terrible, to lose a loved one, to mourn, to dread the existential void. It is, as Lauren Elkin put it, 'a city with a soundtrack in a minor key.' That is well put. 'There is a certain pain, related to love and loss, that it amplifies until it almost feels good.'[2] I have never felt as devastated as I have in Paris, nor have I ever felt that twinge of emotional masochistic savour so hypnotically. Maybe it has to do with the graveyards and the catacombs, the sense that death and darkness lurk around any corner, the sense that the city's surplus of sensuality can decay into something sweetly rotten. Or the sense that the city is hiding something, keeping secrets.

★★★

As I remember it, the Metro train rattled along north towards Montmartre where I was staying in a cheap hostel. It was not even 10 p.m., though, and I did not plan to go back yet. I thought a theatre or cabaret might be next: a Beckett centenary festival was on. Or maybe the streets and nightlife would be theatre enough, even beyond the garishly curated tourist traps in the Latin Quarters and stylish storefronts in the Marais. Even the skulls and femurs of the catacombs were artfully arranged—macabre but lovely, like Théodore Géricault's *The Raft of the Medusa* or performances at the Grand Guignol. Except amidst the stacks of bones, there were what can only be described as prototypes of heart emojis made of skulls and femurs, arranged like a sick joke. Paris is haunted by its undergrounds, its tunnels and skeletal remains, and sewers explored by daring spelunkers, latter-day Situationists.

The original Situationists, Guy Debord's crowd, went 'slipping by night into houses undergoing demolition, hitchhiking nonstop and without destination through Paris during a transportation strike in the name of adding to the confusion, wandering in subterranean catacombs forbidden to the public.'[3] They were like inverted flâneurs, more radical, proto-punk-rock developments of Benjamin's concept of the 'rag-picker' who, at the edge of the curated city, sees the un-curated alleyway, sees the detritus and refuse whereby you can read the dark side of capitalism and bourgeois culture. Here is the invisible city, its backstage, where those too disenfranchised even to be part of the working class linger in doorways and behind dumpsters. I was drawn to dark alleyways but wary of what I might find there.

I thought I might get off the Metro early to catch a show, or who knows, maybe drift into another part of town, and the St-Lazare stop was coming up, as I remember it. But the train did not stop; we flew right through. Where most of the Metro stations were gorgeously tiled, art nouveau masterpieces, this was all exposed wires and pipes, some kind of disaster zone. I can't quite pinpoint why, but whooshing through this exposed station shocked me. It was almost abject, as if I were peaking too deep through a gash in flesh. As if I were seeing the man behind the curtain, the backstage of the city, the sewers beneath the catacombs.

As I turned my head away, I saw my face reflected in the window: translucent, oddly lighted, overlaying the innards of the subway system passing by. In this light it seemed I was not looking at a reflection at all but at the ghost of my father: angular, graven cheeks, a brooding chin, thinning hair made dark auburn through strange downlight. At first I thought of something out of Tadeusz Kantor's Theatre of Death but then I was reminded of that monologue from Sam Shepard's *Buried Child*, when Vince recalls seeing generations back in the facial structure of his reflection in the windshield as he drove through rows of corn. I thought of my father's journeys long ago, maybe on this very route, and how he spoke of Paris when I was a child, how he spoke French to me, how he told me of growing up here, and much later he returned, sleeping over air vents for heat, so long before

I first travelled to the city. Suddenly his suicide the year before mingled with the exposed infrastructure of the St-Lazare station under construction. I was struck by the name: Lazarus, brought back from the dead, still stinking as he walked out of the cave, wrapped like a mummy. What was it like in the days between his death and resurrection?

Those spaces between, beneath, and behind visually curated neighbourhoods—certain dark alleyways, abandoned tunnels, Metro stations under construction—cut through Paris as a kind of exposed theatricality, where the theatre's wall falls, revealing that it was all the time just a painted flat. Every city reveals its invisible infrastructure at times, but there is something about the curated elegance of the inner arrondissements that makes Paris's interruptions feel like a tear in a landscape painting. These interruptions also feel like reminders of the working-class suburbs like Montreuil-sous-Bois (home to the playwright Armand Gatti), ethnically and economically a very different version of the twenty-first-century France. Surrounding the inner arrondissements, these desperately poor but culturally diverse areas are kept out of view of tourists in search of belle-époque views and cafes once frequented by Stein or Picasso.

The train whipped through the station and on through the next. I abandoned my plan to step off, feeling reflective after St-Lazare. I stayed on the Metro and went back to Montmartre. That night it was beautiful out: not too warm, no rain, lots of people outside enjoying the breeze. I drank cheap red wine and ate sausages with people from the hostel. Then, late, we sat on the steps of the eerie white Sacré Couer, maybe until three in the morning. We watched the city lights spread before us like a stage. The City of Lights. A stranger asked me for a light. I stood and reached out my lighter, leaving my bag on the stair, though it held in it my notebooks and passport and camera. It was gone when I turned back. Another man was running, and then the guy with the cigarette ran too. The Egyptian and Canadian from the hostel joined me in chasing them, fruitlessly, down steep steps and over sharp wrought-iron fences. I ended the evening walking aimlessly and out of breath through streets I did not know, wearing torn pants, flagging down police, to whom I tried to tell what happened in broken French and bad charades. I can only imagine how they laughed when I left the station and tried to find my way to the embassy in the last hours before dawn. Of course, American, we will devote all our forces to finding your missing bag and bringing the thieves to justice. You are, after all, our guest. Welcome to Paris. We hope you enjoy your stay.

Notes

1 See the chapter on Émile Zola and Andre Antoine's correspondence in Christopher Innes, *A Sourcebook on Naturalist Theatre* (Routledge, 2002).
2 Lauren Elkin, *Flâneuse: Women Walk the City in Paris, New York, Tokyo, Venice, and London* (Farrar, Straus, and Giroux, 2017), 44.
3 Guy Debord, 'Theory of the Derive' (1958), *Situationist International Anthology*, ed. Ken Knabb (Bureau of Public Secrets, 2012), 53.

9
INVISIBLE CITIES 2

Kyle Gillette: Last year, I remember two in the morning, four in the morning, you were at the monastery and always moving two millimetres at a time, trying dozens of different patterns on the building walls, at different speeds, using different textures.

Vincenzo Sansone: Yes, because the way in which we work with projections is like when Pino works with an actor. We work with improvisations because for us projections are like actors and the space is like the stage. It is the projection that plays on the surface that is the stage. So we have to find the relationship, that is the relationship the actor has with the space. When an actor moves in the space she has to know how to move in the space, you cannot move like in your daily life. And at the same time there is a technique to reach this purpose when you work with projections. So this is the reason I like working with Teatro Potlach, because I can connect my first education, like actor, with my second education. Put them together to create another thing that is—I don't like to call it theatre projections because I think nowadays it's not possible to categorize work—so I like remixing things, put together but not like a collage. To connect them like languages. When we project and for example you see dots. For you they are dots, but if you see the dots together with Daniela—for example, we did this thing in Palermo, in a place associated with ancient Sicilian tuna fishing. And you listen to Daniela who tells this story inside the projections made of white dots upon a red surface; you can image that this is the sea full of blood. The tuna. In that moment could be Daniela inside.

Each time Teatro Potlach mounts *Invisible Cities*, Daniela Regnoli invites spectators to take a journey through a particular city layered with strange sights: acrobats repelling off the sides of monasteries, or walking tightropes, video projections that make old familiar architecture undulate and shape shift or superimpose images of the city's mythic pasts, tunnels made of fabrics that obscure buildings or redirect foot traffic, performances of all sorts placed in alcoves, secret gardens, or hanging out windows of private houses. Depending on each city's history and architecture,

FIGURE 9.1 Marcus Acauan, Pino Di Buduo; photo by Kyle Gillette

elements of the performance can range from the most intimate hand gesture isolated in a small corner to a vast hydraulic platform that emerges from a lake, realizing a local legend of a submerged city. Each performance is different, although some motifs tend to recur. Di Buduo is an anthropologist by training, with a deep respect for architecture and ritual. When he began to recognize the vital links between theatre and anthropology, Di Buduo, in collaboration with the actress Regnoli, dove into rehearsals and training exercises as practices through which to conduct research. He told his former advisor, after he was offered a position that could have led towards becoming a professor at the Sapienza University of Rome, that he would like a year. If during these 12 months Di Buduo could establish a self-sustaining theatre, that would become his research. Otherwise, he would return to academia, a philosophically minded and theatrically oriented anthropologist who asks questions about culture by referring to books and field work.

Although the theatre indeed became self-sustaining, Di Buduo continues to be an anthropologist by intuition. He travels weeks or months ahead of the rest of the group to conduct careful research, to try to glimpse the invisible city—the contours and associations residents may grow to ignore because they have become accustomed to them through daily repetition. He walks the city squares and through alleyways by himself at night, asking questions of residents, watching people walk and interact behind marketplaces or outside places of worship. He reads about old local myths and patterns of daily life—in libraries, certainly, but also in the grooves of well-worn steps, the markings on stone walls. The project has 'as its primary objective to uncover the memory, culture and identity of places,' as the projection artist Sansone puts it.[1] The group's means of uncovering—from projections to cloths to performances—often rely on interruption and novelty, but they are aimed at a kind of memory that will persist deeply after the performance is gone:

> All these interventions bring out from the place a city never seen before, invisible to the eyes of its inhabitants, but present and buried in the meanderings of their memory. The objective is to bring out this memory so that the inhabitants preserve and hand down it to new generations.[2]

Many of the embedded performances in *Invisible Cities* draw out historical layers or local myths, although obliquely, using video patterns or site-specific movement pieces that focus attention on spaces typically neglected or experienced in utilitarian ways.

Some of the work would not normally look like art except for its placement. Di Buduo invites local artisans to do what they normally do at work, but then integrates them—welding, painting, hammering, whittling, cooking, washing, fishing—in odd places throughout the city. These sites frame and open their labour to be seen with fresh eyes. As spectators walk along a prescribed route through the city, everything becomes a potential art object—a cat staring at you, books, a pile of rubble, the moonlight. The pathway is fundamental: like the spine of the body, it forms the central organizing structure of the experience with integrity but flexibility. It also structures the river of experience through which specific details gain significance and gather meaning. Reappropriated bits of the city become defamiliarized, not necessarily by being represented through a distorting lens but through context and juxtaposition.

Teatro Potlach's *Invisible Cities*, like certain Dada and Surrealist artists, implicitly questions the contexts that frame and authorize art. As the aesthetic philosopher Nelson Goodman suggests, the interesting question about art's relationship to reality may not be 'what is art?' but 'when is art?' Goodman offers an example of a pile of rubble that remains invisible or unremarkable in the driveway but whose characteristics become exemplary put into the context of a museum, where patrons expect to see things symbolically or to look at objects more closely. So, Duchamp's ready-mades like *Fountain* become art, do what art does—while simultaneously challenging the very notion of art—not because there is anything intrinsically special about the object but because it is taken from one context and put in another, one with meanings produced by larger dynamics of value, empire, and ideology upon which museums were founded.[3]

In *Great Reckonings in Little Rooms*, Bert States takes up Goodman's insight and thinks about its particular relevance as a question for theatre, where bringing anything from the 'real world' onto the stage, within the proscenium, charges it with a significance and a phenomenal density even before an actor starts overlaying props with particular fictions. Paraphrasing Peter Handke, States notes that onstage 'a chair is a chair pretending to be another chair, and so on,' with the chair's 'pretense' a matter of framing or naming, a fictional spectre.[4] This theatrical sense of semiotic and phenomenological interest is connected to the defamiliarization the Russian formalist critic Viktor Shklosvky sees as fundamental to how art works: art increases 'the difficulty and length of perception because the process of perception is an aesthetic end in itself and must be prolonged.'[5] So art helps us see ourselves seeing, especially in theatre, by attending to what otherwise disappears into networks of causality or meaning-making. When spectators behold familiar objects made strange, they can slow down, attend to the aesthetic energy underlying their travel through the world, and cultivate a quality of attention transportable to the process of daily life.

In a deeply related way, Teatro Potlach defamiliarizes the labour, travel, and public memories of the cities it 'excavates.' It seeks to discover the invisible city and reveal it to its residents. Inspired by Calvino's structure, the performance is built like an archipelago of little cities-within-the-city that spectators can linger over, pass by, or visit at their own pace and through their particular visions. The scenes change based on the traveller's gaze and motion, as the spectator drifts from moment to moment, seeing each building, street, and resident in a new light transformed by surprising juxtapositions and individual or collective memories.

Di Buduo sees the spectator like Marco Polo, making deep contact with cities by moving through them with the eyes of a traveller, though the spectator at times flickers, becomes like Kublai Khan listening, asking questions, and imagining. In Calvino's *Invisible Cities*, the traveller and the emperor understand each other only in part. They do not share a language at first, but Khan fills in the negative space described by Polo's gestures and souvenirs, his cries and songs:

> what enhanced for Kublai every event or piece of news reported by his inarticulate informer was the space that remained around it, a void not filled with words. The descriptions of cities Marco Polo visited had this virtue: you could wander through them in thought, become lost, stop and enjoy the cool air, or run off.[6]

Between Polo's memory and Khan's imagination, between the traveller's performance and the emperor's perception, arose a third city where the spectator was free to roam, to project private desires and understandings.

This freedom was fundamental to Teatro Potlach's *Invisible Cities* from the beginning, even before the group considered performing it in other cities. More than particular images adapted from Calvino's cities, Potlach was inspired by the structure of their telling, the way the reader could linger or jump ahead, the way each site-specific performance offered its own miniature world, the way symbolic relations between the scenes depended on the imagination of a traveller making connections. Though filled with allusions and developed around themes, Potlach rarely makes these into explicit references that fix meaning. Like Calvino's reader, spectators join their perspectives to that of the traveller, the explorer, Marco Polo: 'They become explorers, archaeologists of memory.'[7] The liminal character played by Regnoli mediates between those who walk along the route and those who populate its alcoves.

In 1976, Di Buduo and Regnoli, the anthropologist-director and actress from Rome, moved to Fara in Sabina to start Teatro Potlach. They had travelled the previous year to work with the singular director of Odin Teatret, Eugenio Barba. Regnoli and Di Buduo were struck by the training at Odin, which included gymnastic and acrobatic exercises as well as extended improvisations involving physical and vocal explorations. The founders of Potlach were intrigued with the anthropological possibilities of theatre exercises to connect across cultural rhythms and images. Barba suggested the pair renovate an old crumbling monastery in Fara in Sabina, a remote village less than an hour drive from Rome. It was close enough to Rome to be accessible to artists from Bali to Brazil—and for Potlach to access trains and flights to distant cities—but it was far enough from both the Roman commercial and avant-garde theatre scenes to be a laboratory, a monastery, another world. Soon after, Di Buduo and Regnoli were joined by many other artists, including the Swiss-born Nathalie Mentha who found this work after seeking Odin's summer training. A friend recommended that she journey down to Fara in Sabina to make contact with fellow travellers. She remains still, now more intimately involved than anyone: performing major roles, teaching workshops, organizing festivals and travel opportunities, leading major efforts of the company. During the 1970s and 1980s, projects in South America brought Potlach into contact with South American folk performance traditions, and Argentine and Brazilian performers followed the group back to Rome. This international collection, so close and yet so far from Rome, continues to benefit from its particular proximity. Inevitably, the travellers to see Potlach's work or who participate in workshops end up spending time in Rome, their travels blending in and out of their new meditations on cities. Rome, the city so foundational to Europe, exerts a profound gravitational pull on all the imaginations that travel to and with Teatro Potlach.

Notes

1 Vincenzo Sansone, 'Citta Invisibili of Teatro Potlach: A Journey to Rediscover Our Cultural Heritage', *Handbook of Research on Emerging Technologies for Digital Preservation and Information Modeling* (IGI Global, 2017), 543.
2 Ibid., 536.
3 Nelson Goodman, *Ways of Worldmaking*, v. 51 (Hackett Publishing, 1978).
4 Bert O. States, *Great Reckonings in Little Rooms: On the Phenomenology of Theater* (University of California Press, 1985), 20.
5 Viktor Shklovsky, 'Art as Technique,' *Literary Theory: An Anthology* (1917), 15–21.
6 Calvino, 38.
7 Sansone, 'Citta Invisibili of Teatro Potlach', 100.

10

CITIES AND VIOLENCE

Rome

After you roam all day down the streets and dart between vespas, you can duck into an alleyway that leads into a hidden world: a renaissance courtyard or fifth-century basilica tucked discreetly behind aperitivo bars. These are not separate worlds; they overlap and intertwine. As Freud notes in *Civilization and Its Discontents*, Rome's architecture contains its past versions of itself, but repurposed. Roman epochs sediment in layers of stone. Torn, fragmented, each age simultaneously builds on and represses its predecessors' ruins. In places, an ancient theatre's architecture has forced later buildings to conform to a curve—but then disappeared, leaving an absence described by later developments. In this way Rome is like the individual psyche, and also, Freud extrapolates, civilization itself. A temple to Bacchus or Jupiter retains its foundation but becomes a sacred space for Catholic Mass, re-devoted to Mary, or Paul. The pantheon houses not gods but saints—yet you can feel very well inside that it was not always so. Anyway, it's all since become something else: national patrimony, destinations for sale to tourists, embodiments of power for use in political discourse.

On a hot day, some ancient churches—take the Basilica di Santa Maria in Trastevere—shelter weary travellers with old mosaic floors that wind in spirals and cool dim spaces. Archaeologists join worshippers to retreat from the July heat. In these rooms priests mutter Christian vigils in ancient Latin or medieval Italian, the tongues of Virgil and Dante, cultivating a sanctuary from the hostile pagan Sol. Outside the vines and caper bushes insinuate themselves between ancient cracks. You notice as you roam.

Rome. Roam. Room. The memory of that strange room above the square in Monti, the first place I ever stayed in Rome: a hotel, it turned out, run by Ukrainian Orthodox nuns. At prayer they whispered quickly in lilting Greek rather than Latin. At night, I leaned out the window overlooking the fountain where party people sat on steps and drank Peroni all night, watching each other walk, watching young

FIGURE 10.1 Mass in Rome; photo by Sayna Ghaderi

couples eat gelato, watching tiny cars, the lights, leaving an astonishing heap of mismatched bottles and food scraps, where pigeons descended by the dozen the next morning....

And the next year, in Trastevere, where graffiti scrawled across ancient doorways mingled promiscuously with Catholic iconography and anti-fascist posters—there I stayed in a B&B with starlets of Italian cinema painted above each bed. (I woke up to Anita Ekberg staring down.) Leaving one morning I tripped down the stairs, my eye on an empty wheelchair in the corner by the door. (I was busy wondering how the wheelchair-bound fared in this city of stairways and hills.) I fell hard and hobbled with difficulty to a kiosk where the owner refused to take a 50-euro note for a bottle of water and then chased me down the street, calling the polizia over because he insisted I took a vengeful photo on my phone. Which I didn't. I asked if that was illegal anyway—no laws seem to obtain here regarding driving or parking, but this?—to which the polizia answered the heat was getting to the poor guy's head. Fair enough. It was a hot dry summer and everyone seemed crazed. The fountains and spigots flowed like oases in the desert.

The driest thirst, the cruellest sun, the gauchest spectacle was in the lines near the Vatican, where Pakistani tour-sellers intercepted tourists of every imaginable nationality to hawk unofficial guided walks. (When I travelled with Sayna Ghaderi, the Iranian photographer whose images of Rome appear in this chapter, she took an Indian tour guide's picture; the tour guide waved his finger, 'no.')

But the Vatican museums were nothing but cameras and phones pointed every direction, just like St. Peter's Basilica: the sacred as the image-mine, plundered by pilgrims from a hundred thousand cities. Papa Francesco wasn't there this

64 Cities and violence: Rome

FIGURE 10.2 Vatican City; photo by Sayna Ghaderi

Wednesday to give his address, but some still gathered, not knowing this was his month off. In the Sistine Chapel, the voices were deafening. A voice came over the loudspeaker every two or three minutes to say: *Silencio. Quiet Please. No photo, no video.* This was followed by a moment of relative silence, then the din of two dozen different languages whispered by hundreds rose steadily to another climax, when the loudest voice of all returned: *Silencio. Quiet Please. No photo, no video.* This went on all day, every day. Meanwhile the German couple next to me snuck photos using the front-facing selfie cameras on their Korean phones. Afterwards a cabdriver, a Roman from birth, decried the gilded palace of thieves as he drove along the Tiber, spitting about the Church's blasphemy against its poor. Jesus wouldn't recognize it, he said. For St. Augustine, Rome was also the antithesis to his imagined *City of God*, but it held that utopia's promise in its unsacked churches, spared miraculously by marauding Goths. Too, Rome's grandeur and centrality and civic liveliness offered a worldly metaphor for that otherworldly, potential city, infinity's city. And it does go on. And on and on. Its infinity is shocking except that it all feels familiar too, like you've seen it before. In the Piazza della Repubblica and the Piazza Venezia, in the Trevi Fountain: the strange glitz and cinematic otherworlds of Federico Fellini's *8½* (1963) and *Roma* (1972), or Paolo Sorrentino's *The Great Beauty* (2013). In the ruins and wrecks of war, the traumatized neorealism of Roberto Rossellini's films like *Rome, Open City* (1945). But also monuments and obelisks and train stations inexplicably gleaming as a fascist legacy—including the Centro Sperimentale di Cinematografia and Cinecittá, the school and studio that nurtured Italian film. All rationalist fascist lines, the same

FIGURE 10.3 Piazza di Santa Maria in Trastevere, Rome; photo by Kyle Gillette

as much of Rome. Like Mussolini was just another cruel emperor, no worse than a Nero or Caligula. Just a phase, just part of the city's evil history. Then on the outskirts, down by the sea, far beyond the Antonine Wall, the fringes of society. This is the world of Paolo Pasolini, a world of prostitutes and drug addicts and murder on the beach. The Rome that doesn't partake of ancient empires or medieval cathedrals or mid-century modern glamour. The Rome of roamers, of Sardinians and North Africans, the Rome invisible to three-day itineraries. Neighbourhoods that might as well be different cities rub up against each other in crooked, twisted juxtaposition. Every time there seems to be a wall delineating the city's boundaries, the streets and houses continue beyond, expansive, expanding, infinite. Rome's tributaries and trade routes, its sphere of political and cultural influence follow the journeys out of the city up to the Sabine hills and down to Fiumicino and across the Mediterranean.

Rome once, of course, went much further. This city was for a millennium, the mad jumbled beating heart of the world's greatest empire. Britain to Egypt, Austria to Palestine. A world where togas, villas, and wine circulated to improbable landscapes, where stone theatres united cities built along rigid Roman grids. Across continents cities became extensions of *this* city, not the oldest city but the one from which culture and law would radiate outwards. At least, after Rome devoured the culture of Athens, Jerusalem, Alexandria, digested them, reconstituted them, pushed all out to the provinces in stone pastiche. Rome founded Bologna and Florence, and Venice, Paris, Lyon, Seville, Barcelona, Salzburg, Cologne, Zurich, Strasbourg, Geneva, Ljubljana, Dubrovnik, London, Dover, York.... Cities whose ancient ruins persist in walled-off courtyards with informative placards. Where streets are paved over Roman roads. Where baths still draw pilgrims and tourists together. Cities where theatres and courts embodied culture and law for 2000 years.

Rome never en-gridded itself though. A city of labyrinths and narrow alleyways and the original ghetto, it refused to succumb to the order imprinted elsewhere. Its unfolding was determined by the river and the hills, not the master plan of conquerors. Untamable, Rome was yet the wild heart of civilization. It spread its spectacles in part through garb, in part through circuses and theatres reproduced in the heart of client and colony cities. Meanwhile its own theatres sucked spectacles of difference in from the provinces to glorify and entertain the citizens. Egyptian obelisks and Athenian columns were brought in to build piazzas; a flooded Coliseum restaged victorious sea battles against Carthage; giraffes and foreign gods arrived, swallowed by spectacle, performing Rome, the capital city of the world.

European auditoriums and theatres bear the lasting imprints of Rome's orientation between seers and scenes. The director Romeo Castellucci calls the Italianate theatrical space, which has imprinted its spectacular structure on thousands of city's theatres, coercive in its demand that something must appear before spectators' hungry eyes. Even

> the layout of the auditorium, with the different levels one above another, is belligerent, like in the Roman circus. There is no possibility of passage or circulation between the audience and the stage, there's a clear separation. It's a space that belongs completely to the city, a civic space.[1]

It does not belong to the artists, not to the individuals, certainly not to the foreigners, but to the city itself. But what is the city itself? The space where decrees might be proclaimed? Where gladiators do battle, sometimes from ships, where conquered barbarian kings and elephants and concubines can be paraded from the far shores? The power of the spectacle underlies the power of the city.

Audacious bodies specially robed demand attention, or have performances demanded of them, insisted on by demanding eyes. The demand suffuses everything: the Pantheon and Coliseum, the Fellini landmarks, the theatres, the al fresco cafes, the people watching small concerts by the river. The speeches of political leaders and popes, the surprises waiting around corners. The blood spilled in front of spectators, the parades welcoming conquering generals and football heroes. The exotic animals at the zoo. The tourists. The busking modern gladiators wearing togas or capes, charging tourists for selfies; for extra, they re-enact the assassination of Julius Caesar using small wooden swords.

The city as experienced by the traveller is inextricable from its preserved ruins. Yet what is preserved is not the fallen Rome of caesars, nor of medieval churches and renaissance palaces, but rather Rome's very ruination. The Coliseum, to take perhaps the most theatrical example, is far from a restored return to the days of

FIGURE 10.4 Coliseum; photo by Sayna Ghaderi

gladiators. Though it was recently power-washed to a more antiseptic shade of off-white, the crumbling exterior is the very thing that testifies to its age; the patina of fallen-ness lies at the heart of its status as a modern attraction and historic monument. It's unthinkable to restore it the way the Vatican restored St. Peter's Basilica. Ancient Rome can only ever be restored to a point; otherwise its ruins would lose the mark of feeling long ago and far away, alien and fallen, twisted, traumatized. What is being retained, preserved, theatricalized, is not Ancient Rome at all but only its fall.

Tourists travel between the old buildings of Rome, in effect, to dwell among its decay, even as we drink Negroni and listen to symphonies or see theatre. This might be a form of slow-motion disaster tourism. We go as inheritors of Rome's Law, its cultural assimilation of Hellenistic philosophy and architecture and literature, but we are not Romans. Rome did not give Europe its modern cities. They rose, rather, from the ashes of the empire's disintegration. Like the buildings that surround and emerge from ruins left half-standing in the old city, these cities grew up among the wreckage, were born of destruction. When we go back as tourists to Rome, we go not as Romans but Barbarians.

Note

1 Romeo Castellucci, in Joe Kelleher, Nicholas Ridout, Claudia Castellucci, Chiara Guidi, and Romeo Castellucci, *The Theatre of Sociétas Raffaello Sanzio* (Routledge, 2007), 204.

11

CITIES AND DECEPTION

Las Vegas

When you arrive in Las Vegas by plane, you can just barely spot something garish below in the sand. If you fly in at night, the artificial lights cut a scar across the natural dark. Even in twilight, harsh pinks and neon blues tear a gash across the desert. For the traveller who arrives by car, the horizon glows like sunset in the distance, or a radioactive mirage. It expands as you approach—until it swallows you, and all you see is light.

The city baffles with gauche spectacles of desire and risk. But the city is also impossible to ignore: as Venturi, Brown, and Izenour suggest in *Learning from Las Vegas*, the Strip replaces modern architecture with a jumbled madness of kitsch and symbolism, which 'includes at all levels,' drawing diverse signs together in startling juxtapositions. Unlike the cohesive modernism of Chicago's Magnificent Mile, the Strip 'is not an order dominated by the expert and made easy for the eye'; it epitomizes, in its collision of incongruous signs, postmodern pastiche. More, 'if you take the signs away, there is no place.'[1] And what do the signs signify? How does the traveller read them?

On the Strip many hotels and casinos are stage sets of other cities. The skyline is a surreal jumble of skyscrapers, medieval castle towers, pyramids, the Statue of Liberty, the Eiffel Tower. Outside, the palatial buildings are hard to pin down, dominated by neon, amplifying the lure of desire. Inside, the Venetian reproduces a canal complete with singing gondoliers, lined with shops and al fresco cafes. The sky above, lit blue, creates negative space that outlines faux rooftops. In the faux St. Mark's Square, faux actors from another time perform faux commedia scenarios in masks and stilts, singing, juggling, repeating each afternoon at 4 p.m. sharp just in front of the Pandora store. The gelato shop stands next to the rococo bridge over the chemically blue water (stinking not of Venetian decomposition but antiseptic chlorine); the shop offers dozens of flavours, an exaggeration of desires on sale in the old-world Venice. Down the road, the Bellagio's fountains dance in computerized synchronicity, entertaining people drinking cocktails inside Lago or Le Cirque—high rollers acting like carefree aristocrats on the Riviera—or the tourists who gather near the artificial lake across the street from Paris. Paris sports round cafe tables and slot machines around the base of the Eiffel Tower, which rises up through the cloudy sky-ceiling to soar above the Strip. Nearby New York, New York reproduces city streets in miniature, a roller-coaster rattling over its replica delis and around the Statue of Liberty.

Even the casinos without indexical mappings of known cities create miniature cities of sorts, like oversized snow globes collected on a crowded shelf. Unmoored by particular geographical referents, Planet Hollywood crystallizes the simulacrum of movie images and celebrity itself without resembling Los Angeles landmarks in any concrete way. Excalibur creates an immersive theatrical vision of Arthurian legend, liberated from appeals to real English geography. The Luxor is pure Orientalism à la Edward Said: ancient Egyptian pyramids and the Sphinx and camels exoticized as theatrical fantasies of the ancient and nonwestern other. Caesar's Palace invokes an ancient Rome that never existed—but that magnifies every tendency the classical Hollywood imagination ascribes to emperors and orgies.

Other casinos stage virtual cities without reference to concrete geography: the MGM Grand, the most aptly named Mirage. Or they double up on performance as a reason for being, like Circus Circus. As Hunter S. Thompson described in a mescaline, LSD- and ether-fused binge immortalized in *Fear and Loathing in Las Vegas*, Circus Circus amplifies the tawdry performances that bring these casinos to life:

> The ground floor is full of gambling tables, like all the other casinos [...] but the place is about four stories high, in the style of a circus tent, and all manner of strange County-Fair/Polish Carnival madness is going on up in this space. Right above the gambling tables the Forty Flying Carazito Brothers are doing a high-wire trapeze act, along with four muzzled Wolverines and the Six Nymphet Sisters from San Diego [...] so you're down on the main floor playing blackjack, and the stakes are getting high when suddenly you chance to look up, and there, right smack above your head is a half-naked fourteen-year-old girl being chased through the air by a snarling wolverine.[2]

The audacious, tawdry circus display—complete with female objectification, danger to the innocent, animal violence, Roman excess, the carnivalesque—touches on something fundamental to Las Vegas, and through it, the twisted hypocrisies of the American dream.

> Psychedelics are almost irrelevant in a town where you can wander into a casino any time of the day or night and witness the crucifixion of a gorilla—on a flaming neon cross that suddenly turns into a pinwheel, spinning the beast around in wild circles above the crowded gambling action.[3]

It becomes hard to separate the acid-fuelled hallucinations of Thompson's 'gonzo journalism' from the disorienting psychedelic displays embedded in the casinos.

Over the past few decades, the still mob-ruled mid-century vibe of Thompson's 1972 Vegas has given way to a slicker, more streamlined corporate Strip, but still you can see in the very texture of the spectacles the dark underbelly of late capitalism's most brutal consumerist gaze, sexual objectifications, gambling excesses, crimes, cruelties.

Vegas is home to an elaborate and terrible theatre scene: stages for musical tours from Broadway, but also several regular Cirque du Soleil shows, burlesque cabarets, and music acts frozen in time, like Donny and Marie Osmond or Celine Dion. This is where expensive, technologically astonishing spectacles can happen excessively, guaranteed a constant circulation of new spectators willing to spend hundreds of dollars on scenic fireworks. It is where sex can be performed and sold outwardly, unabashedly, with gusto—and glitter. Las Vegas stages are where once-original music acts go to die—or worse, to become undead zombie versions of what they once were. Here performers, and the whole entertainment industrial complex, undermine any sense that performance is necessarily more singular, immediate, or intimate than film or television. What happens in Vegas stays in Vegas, they say, and that idealized hermetic seal from the rest of the world permits spectacular depravity, theatrical decay, deadly virtuality, the male gaze amplified many times over. In Vegas, the sensitive viewer can understand why Plato might want to banish theatre, why the early Christians saw it as the work of the devil.

I was last in Las Vegas for the Association for Theatre in Higher Education conference at the beginning of August 2017. Coming out of a meeting with the editor of this book, I felt excited about its possibilities, so I indulged with a lunch in Paris and a journey through several Italian cities. This was only a couple weeks after I had returned from a month in the real Italy, so the concentration and reduction at work in Vegas felt particularly surreal. Exiting one casino and entering another, I was struck by the miniaturized, inverted Grand Tour of it all: token variety without historic specificity; apparent differences masking fundamental sameness. Each time I moved between casinos I passed briefly into 110°F heat, only to re-enter sliding glass doors into a new air-conditioned, extra-oxygenated spectacle (the better to keep gamblers awake). Each little microcosm advertised difference, adding up to the Strip's gaudy display of superficial variety, but inside each roulette and blackjack table or slot machine blurred into one vast machine. Here, beneath all the apparent diversity: the real point of it all, the contingent yet financially consequential game at the heart of the city.

Two months later, on the first of October, spectators gathered at the outdoor Las Vegas Village music venue near Mandalay Bay and the Luxor to hear country music bands perform as part of the Route 91 Harvest festival. As singer Jason Aldean stood on the stage for the festival's final act, a shooter fired hundreds of rounds into the crowd from a window in the Mandalay Bay hotel. He killed 58 people, wounding another over 400 with bullets and causing injuries to 869 in all.[4] This gross violation of public space and harm to individual spectators shredded the implicit bond of cultural gatherings, where people expect to experience performance together peacefully. At the same time, the frequency of American mass shootings limited the nation's shock at this event to a few weeks. To be vulnerable to harm by military-style assault rifle fire while participating in a gathering for performance belies the wealth and privilege of American cities. Compared to Aleppo or Baghdad, Las Vegas is quite safe, a place where civilization (of a sort) flourishes, where an industry productively redirects base desires and aggressions into financial profit. Yet something sinister lies in the cultural violence one can see in the whole economy of Vegas—hungry gazes, excessive consumption, reckless risk. The shooter was a high roller recently down on his luck and into depraved online viewing. The flip side of the American dream, in all its materialism, acquisitiveness, and addiction to spectacle, is this nightmare.

Notes

1. Robert Venturi, Denise Scott Brown, and Steven Izenour, *Learning from Las Vegas* (MIT Press, 1977), 53.
2. Hunter Stockton Thompson, *Fear and Loathing in Las Vegas: A Savage Journey to the Heart of the American Dream* (Vintage, 2010), 46.
3. Ibid., 190.
4. Mark Berman, 'Las Vegas police end investigation into massacre without "definitively" determining what motivated the gunman' *The Washington Post*, August 3, 2018.

12

INVISIBLE CITIES 3

Daniela Regnoli: This work [performing in the streets of the city] teaches us to be so concrete. It is very unteachable, but if the difficulties are not there I have to invent difficulties.
Kyle Gillette: Because difficulties are what make something concrete?
DR: Exactly, so you find that when I say resistance, okay, everyone understands the word but then what I have to do is find a resistance in my action. I demonstrate now my effort because this is the representation of the resistance [Regnoli demonstrates a shift of physical tensions] where you have to go to make that concrete, that helps you to find the resistance. And so all these difficulties test you, no? To put your work in different situations to resolve it and to find the concreteness, you see? To be concrete in a work like Invisible Cities, *for example… I imagine from the side of Pino, he has wonderful ideas—'I would like to make this and that'—and if he's not concrete in the situation he will be completely lost. Maybe he does not find an adaptation to the situation, I mean not to remain fixed to what maybe could be his idea and say okay I can't do it so maybe I do it a little bit less. No; he has to put his idea, if he has one, in relation with the concrete problem and see how the two dialogue. Maybe this: in the work, you discover another possibility that you didn't think of before.*

Beginning over four decades ago, the members of Teatro Potlach, gathered from across Europe, Asia, and South America, trained from early in the morning and people came to Fara in Sabina to see their strange performances late in the evening. They worked in a converted monastery, but also in city streets and down the hillside. Spectators travelled from all around: from Rome, of course, but also Denmark, Hungary, Brazil, and Bali—anywhere, it seemed, besides Fara in Sabina. The residents of Fara have always been suspicious of outsiders, and with good reason: Etruscans, Romans, Lombards, and others have threatened this hill before, and much of the village's oldest architecture is devoted to gaining vantage points from which a large boulder might be rolled down onto approaching invaders. Fara in Sabina's twin monasteries—one of silent sisters, the others of sisters who spoke—long embodied the people's preference for seclusion. The Sabine residents in the 1970s, whose mothers' mothers' mothers lived in the same houses, were suspicious of this young theatre company during its early years. They whispered rumours: Teatro Potlach was a cult, a radical utopian political commune, a place for sex orgies. The few who ventured to spy rehearsals saw something surprising in its concreteness: physical and vocal exercises, repetitions of songs and movement scores, simple hard work.

Then, in 1992, Teatro Potlach created a performance that would be for the residents of Fara in Sabina—not just a festival but a journey, not only a spectacle but a city-wide encounter: between travellers and residents, between the theatre and the city, between art and life. Di Buduo worked with the company and local associations to create an event that involved everyone who lived there, worked there, ate and celebrated and mourned there. Choirs, orchestras, acrobats, craftswomen and craftsmen, architectural experts, historians, anthropologists, people who owned interesting houses, who made wine or olive oil from vineyards and trees that grew in the surrounding hills and valleys—these groups and families collaborated, even opened their homes to a course through town. Each performance or installation became something like one of Calvino's cities unto itself. They all added up to a kind of exposure to the hidden world of work and life in Fara in Sabina, the invisible city. In subsequent years, this encounter blossomed into a meaningful and abiding relationship. People began to share their homes with festival participants from five continents. Residents walked up the steep steps to the theatre at the top of the town to see bold multimedia experiments and anthropologically rich intercultural encounters between Asian, South American, and European practices. Art and labour and life blended, entwined.

Over the past 27 years, each iteration of this performance has unfolded distinctively, drawing from the particular anthropology, geography, and history of the city where it was created. When the second *Invisible Cities* happened in Klagenfurt, Austria the year after the first one in Fara in Sabina, geographic differences gave birth to differences in approach to theatrical research. Teatro Potlach was not on home turf. Instead, it played the role of a caravan of travellers removed from local customs to sustain them but (perhaps) capable of seeing dynamics invisible to everyday inhabitants of the host city. Klagenfurt was the opposite of Fara in Sabina's narrow medieval alleyways, steep streets, and closely huddled old buildings. The space was dominated rather by a lake, a wide canal, and a castle. So Di Buduo learned from locals about a myth of a city sunk into this lake. Engineers helped Teatro Potlach build a platform that hydraulically lifted from beneath the surface of the water. The canal, an artificial and relatively recent addition to the town, was covered over with cloths. These scenic elements, along with the content of the performances, derived from the history and geography of Klagenfurt's particular dynamics. And so it would be elsewhere: 'Each location is unique, the medieval village of Fara Sabina suggests a different exchange from the lake at Klagenfurt, or the abandoned dock where the Liverpool event is to take place.'[1] In Rovereto, the work of the native son and futurist artist Fortunato Depero was projected onto columns. In Tehran, an old political prison was reanimated through projections and performances, including by its former inmates.

Yet, over time certain images and leitmotifs sometimes repeated, although in different forms (tightropes, repelling harnesses, vast cloths, angel wings, video projections of particular patterns). These recurrent images connect cities by association, layering a kind of unconscious migration into the work visible to any spectator or participant who followed from city to city. When in 2016 Potlach performed *Invisible Cities* again in Fara in Sabina for the first time in 25 years, the performance carried home the afterimages of its journeys across the world, to Klagenfurt, Rovereto, Lecce Braga, Fontenais-sous-Bois, Holstebro, Liverpool, Londrina, Mazatlán, San Antonio, Tehran, and so many other cities.

Does Teatro Potlach still carry the paradigm of that first *Invisible Cities* performance, and the life of Fara in Sabina, to those foreign cities it researches and temporarily transforms? In one sense the company resembles Marco Polo from Calvino's novel. The Great Khan asks about the traveller's native Venice: why, he asks, does Polo never mention it? The explorer responds that every time he speaks of these cities he says something about Venice. Venice raised the explorer Polo, constituting his first coordinates of the mysteries of urban life. Just as Polo carries Venice with him, Teatro Potlach surely carries a trace of Fara in Sabina with it wherever it goes, or so it seems: even if only as the medieval, narrow-alleyed labyrinth against which all other cities appear variously remarkable or familiar.

But then I asked Di Buduo, Regnoli, Mentha, and others if the group's excavations can be seen as extrapolations from this hometown—if Fara in Sabina was their Venice. They all said no. Despite nearly half a century in this village, no one is from here, and most members prefer to live in nearby towns or hillside orchards. Di Buduo, Regnoli, and Irene Rossi first encountered urban life in Rome, but matured through contact with many other cities; for the projection artist Sansone it was Palermo; for Mentha it was Geneva; Zsofia Gyulas brings Budapest; Marcus Acuan Rio de Janeiro; Gustavo Riondet Buenos Aires. Teatro Potlach's presence in Fara in Sabina was from the beginning an encounter and interlayering of memories of other cities, including the everyday and theatrical practices artists developed elsewhere before moving here.

Once Barba advised Regnoli and Di Buduo to go to Fara in Sabina, to make a theatre out of an old and crumbling monastery, the co-founders began to infuse the village with new, diverse life. As artists from Bali to Brazil joined them, Fara became marked by the sharing of international cultures in a way it had never quite been. Yet travelling had always been an important aspect of Fara's identity, as this spot formed an important stop on ancient salt roads, on the Cammino di San Francesco, and as a trading post near important rivers, including the Farfa and even the Tiber. As a long-time node that never became a huge metropolis, Fara in Sabina is not so much the city that shaped Potlach in the way that Venice shaped Marco Polo; rather, it establishes the laboratory wherein Potlach researched what underlies the lives of cities as such, wherein the theatre group rehearsed what a city might be. Then, as these artists began to travel together, encountering cities around the world, the members of Teatro Potlach brought something of the confluence of Fara in Sabina with them—one made of so many personal and cultural ghosts, so many intersecting influences. This little city helped Di Buduo and others see what lurked within foreign urban fabrics with fresh eyes: vision via juxtaposition. After two and a half decades, Potlach also brought parts of those cities it engaged back to inhabit its home town. The 25th anniversary performance was also infused with the journeys of festival participants from all over the world, artists who would bring their own cities with them into this one.

Along with its lived, decades-long urban anthropology, Potlach developed aesthetic intuitions drawn from travel and contacts between highbrow and popular culture, archaic foreign traditions, and familiar contemporary Italian innovations. Both Di Buduo and Regnoli grew up in a Rome still steeped in the post-war avant-garde and the spectacles of Giorgio Strehler. This experimentalism infused their sensibilities, and stretched far beyond Rome to other European influences such as Meyerhold, Artaud, Brecht, and Beckett. The legacy of the avant-garde as well as that of mid-century epic theatre is present across the group's scenographic visions, its actor training, and its textual affinities. Potlach's 2010 adaptation of Jules Vernes' *20,000 Leagues Under the Sea* (still among the most popular and requested production in its repertory) explores the relationship between video projections and the presence of the performer with a sophistication and care that—on the surface—resembles visual worlds of Robert LePage, John Jesurun, or even the Wooster Group.

Yet there is a popular, even folksy flavour to the work at odds with the avant-garde too. *20,000 Leagues Under the Sea*, for example, includes sophisticated, multi-layered video projection experiments (designed by Stefano Di Buduo, Pino's son); they are strange and haunting, involving intricate layering of projectors, transparent surfaces, and live performance to create floating sea creatures and a bold aesthetic. Yet the production appeals to very young children too. Teatro Potlach's work can feel approachable and popular in such a way that includes not only old folktales or myths but also the twentieth century's technologically disseminated culture: Hollywood and Cinecittá, rock and jazz. Regnoli grew up in a cinematic family; she imagined worlds as a child beneath a table while her father wrote screenplays for major Roman studios. (This space beneath the table, this theatre of possibility, was Regnoli's Venice, she said.) Di Buduo walked to the cinema almost every day growing up. Their cinematic influences tend towards the aesthetically high-minded and experimental. One of the group's performances, *Fellini's Dream*, is essentially a pastiche of the film-maker's famous images, while the music from *8½* begins every *Invisible Cities* procession.

Yet, even with these quotations, adaptations, and affinities for Fellini, Teatro Potlach's worlds rarely feel challenging or opaque. Even in Potlach's most postmodern fragmented performances and its boldest images, I never get that sense of shocking otherworldliness I see in the work of Socìetas Raffaello Sanzio or the intricate deconstructions of live action and video in the work of William Forsythe. Rather, at a Teatro Potlach performance I feel warmly invited into a festival space where aesthetic energy gathers and diffuses unevenly within the fabric of the city. The physical, unmediated work of the actor blends with an organic integration of video. Even the video projections and intricate sound-mixing are approached as if by an actor or musician. Sansone leans not on only on advanced software to create video mapping, wherein images precisely overlay building facades, he becomes projectionist-as-actor; he spends long nights with Di Buduo adjusting and readjusting in the street, in a physically intimate engagement with the space.

Teatro Potlach does not easily fit into the circulations of commercial theatre or the scenes of experimental theatre; its spectacles are as far from Broadway and the West End as they are from the Festival d'Avignon or Under the Radar. In many ways Potlach rebels against, or rather retreats from, both. The group is perhaps best described by what Barba famously termed 'the third theatre': one that 'lives on the fringe, often outside or on the outskirts of the centers and capitals of culture.'[2] This is a theatre whose members train exhaustively and in direct contact with older traditions but without professional academies or family lineages that pass on conventions. The work seems essential, warmly approachable, connected to folk rituals and daily life as much as to Italian theatrical traditions such as opera and commedia dell'arte and cinematic history. Barba's Odin Teatret in Denmark operates this way: radically intercultural yet deeply rooted, on the 'outskirts of the centers and capitals of culture' yet conversant with their developments, drawn from old forms of ritual and at the same time steeped in the legacy of influential director-theorists such as Stanislavski (the Russian father of modern realism), Meyerhold (his one-time acolyte turned constructivist and pioneer of biomechanics), Brecht (the German director and playwright who most deeply influenced western notions of estrangement), and especially, Grotowski (the Polish director and theorist whose research went ever further and deeper into exploring unmediated human encounters). These figures and others represent to Teatro Potlach an orientation towards research, not commercial or even artistic advancement. Added to these influences, Barba's work, which made a profound early impression on Di Buduo, Regnoli, and Mentha, was engaged in a kind of intercultural anthropology. The point was not to create something beautiful or shocking or new, but—through theatre—more deeply to investigate culture, behaviour, being.

The structure, and name, of Teatro Potlach comes from the gift festivals of Pacific Northwestern Native American societies. At potlatch festivals since long before the arrival of European colonizers, participating tribes gave gifts to other tribes; in return the receiver gave something of even greater value—understood less as quantified desire and production than spiritual and cultural significance. Sometimes huge bonfires burned gifts into an excessive gesture of giving without any remainder while performances of drumming and dance went on into the night. Di Buduo's conception of the company's roots in the potlatch resembles the barters, or cultural exchange, so vital to his friend and mentor Barba. In Barba's work, spectators see images laced with traces of deep myths, intercultural exchanges, songs, and movements bartered between far-flung peoples marked by radical difference yet related devotions to tradition.

Barba entered theatrical research in the wake of Grotowski's groundbreaking laboratory theatre. He collaborated closely with Grotowski in Poland in the 1960s, learning deeply from his precise physical and probing way of working. He became Grotowski's assistant director for such historically important projects as *Akropolis* and even edited and published his influential book *Towards a Poor Theatre*. Along with Barba's incorporation of Indian Kathakali dance traditions, Grotowski's influence was fundamental to Odin Teatret's early work in the late 1960s and early 1970s. Grotowski's work often incorporated old songs and simple physical improvisations that could reveal something authentic and subtle beneath masks of culture. Grotowski sought to pick up where Stanislavski left off, driving beneath 'realistic' representations to the essence of real actions and the authentic encounters of human beings responding to each other without mediation, without the masks of cultural identity. Since the late 1960s, Grotowski's legacy has led to practices as divergent from each other—and from his later work embodied in the Workcenter of Jerzy Grotowski and Thomas Richards in Pontedera—as Grotowski's Poor Theatre was from Stanislavski's Moscow Art Theatre. Barba's branch of this tree has led increasingly towards intercultural exchanges, deep Jungian source images, and festive processions.

At Odin Teatret, processions and festivals play a major role in extending theatre into the town of Holstebro and putting it into contact with the wider world. The nine-day-and-night Festuge, staged through the streets and buildings of Holstebro, involves both local institutions and traditions and foreign artists from many cultures. Like a parade through town streets and public buildings the performers flow—some dancing, others walking, in recent years some on horseback, some wearing tribal headdresses. The Festuge pours international performance traditions through the small Danish city, rubbing cultures against each other—spilling finally into broad grassy clearings or along the shores of the lake. Odin's work has long been built on this kind of intercultural exchange between performers. A centrepiece of Barba's approach, 'barters' between the travelling players of Odin Teatret and villages all over the world staged exchanges: of songs, dances, stories, ways of working.

While distinct cultures come together through juxtaposed songs, texts, images, and symbols, Barba's direction rigorously focuses on the actor's core physical presence. The actor's precise work brings concrete practice to the laboratory space, putting one embodied cultural background into contact with others through reduction to essential features. In his 1994 book *The Paper Canoe*, Barba outlines the ways performers 'can reduce an action to its essence, to its impulse. They know how to distil each sequence, keeping only the essential actions.'[3] In this way, action can embody memory to penetrate 'beneath the skin of the times and to find the numerous paths which lead to our origins.'[4] While the quality that elevates Odin Teatret's performers comes from an abundance of energy and switching between cultural forms, it depends on omission of excess and finding points of equilibrium between imbalance and tension. Barba admired the presence of actors in several Asian performance traditions, the way 'extra-quotidian' methods of standing with bent knees or walking from a place of imbalance can force the performer to engage in greater physical commitment. The body is full of potential: it has the freedom that comes from reduction, a pliable readiness to change, to respond. Then this readiness allows actors from different traditions to exchange songs and dances or physical forms, awake to each other's core, to minute shifts in posture or energy. The shift between one moment and another, one culture and another, can then awaken a liminal space with maximal freedom. Barters, deriving from an old medieval European conception of community, form the basis for Barba's practice of cultural exchange.

Teatro Potlach's approach to the archaeology of cities and the role of the actor in mediating cultural exchange is deeply connected to the barters of Barba's Odin Teatret. Di Buduo and other members regularly collaborate with Odin. Barba continues to teach workshops every year as part of F.L.I.P.T., where he works to get to the skeleton of participants' proposals. Potlach's own workshops have this in common. Regnoli, after leading a workshop in 2017, spoke to me of the freedom in the actor she, Di Buduo, Mentha, and others teach as a kind of potentiality open to the world, to whatever might happen. Referring to the 'Lightness' Calvino points to in *Six Memos for the New Millennium*, this freedom is hard-won. Calvino's examples include texts by Ovid and Kafka that work by reducing weight, liberating language, but his lessons relate to the work of the actor for Potlach. Effort is required to produce freedom and lightness—like the bird whose flapping wings depend on physical commitment and concrete engagement with resistance. Along with 'Quickness,' 'Exactitude,' 'Visibility,' and 'Multiplicity,' 'Lightness' as understood by Calvino infuses the thought of Teatro Potlach, not as a guideline but a fundamental coordinate of creativity, as a force engaged in opposites—through which cultures might more deeply, elementally encounter one another.

But Potlach's approach to incorporating elemental performance research into intercultural contact is also reoriented from Odin's approach: based less on the metaphor of barter than of gift. Both barter and gift economies predate modern capitalism and early monetary cultures. They rely not on abstraction, quantitative value, and alienation but intimate exchanges rooted to the physical world, to culture and use. The barter economy (wherein goods and services are traded directly) is however a recognizable precursor to capitalism: it is based on exchange and equilibrium, efficiencies of commerce. A gift, or potlatch, economy is something else. The very connection between communities, individual desire, use value, and the purpose of work in the utopian descriptions of potlatch societies is fundamentally connected to the sharing of surplus. Anthropological theories by Georges Bataille and Marcel Mauss suggest a deeply human, passionate, and even 'magical' element to the potlatch, which is animated by sacrifice and an exuberant energy of transcending the self.[5]

This sense of a gift economy underlies Teatro Potlach's approach, or at least its ideal. Rather than the equilibrium of exchange, the company's work and its relationship to the cities it inhabits are often excessive, overstretched, irrepressible, and even irresponsible—as if resources were infinite, as if to create must always to pour water down the mountain, watching it cascade, or to shine light: just because the surplus energy is there, just because its presence radiates into a rich, vivid world. Like its namesake potlatch festivals of Northwestern Native American tribes, this theatre's moments of contact do not seek to match but always exceed. The massive scale of the performance pieces, seemingly performing the entire city sometimes, feels like the most generous and audacious surplus shared without the expectation of exchange. Not that the giving is in one direction, from artists to residents; Di Buduo's attitude to the cities Potlach travels to is marked by curiosity, openness, a sense of wonder in discovering each place's buried stories. The residents do give back, except that even to say it that way misses the point. The reciprocity here is not a matter of exchange anymore. It better resembles ancient practices of hospitality. The very distinction between groups who might represent different interests or values dissolves into an intercultural city. Everyone is invited into a powerful state of mutual giving.

Sharing surplus has always been fundamental to Potlach's process. The group was particularly influenced by its early travels through South America, its encounters with rituals and parades in Brazil and Argentina, where music, dance, and their extensions into the streets and forests broke down distinctions between art and life. Teatro Potlach has created its own processions through city streets, channelling the energy of these practices into new ones. Inverted, with spectators becoming the river that moves through the city, the course of *Invisible Cities* maintains something of that carnival parade encounter. Performance pours through the city, expecting nothing in return except the experience of the journey.

The origin of *Invisible Cities* lies in Potlach's desire not only to 'give the city back to its residents,' but in fact to include them as participants and to draw from their deep lived experience, their daily performances of culture. People bring their work to Di Buduo as gifts too. He then places these propositions back in the city—in the alcoves, the old churches, the passageways—framing people's performances but showing the inside of the work rather than its products. The potters do not show their wares, which immediately implicates them in ownership and commerce; rather, Di Buduo situates the journey such that spectator-travellers observe the labour of pottery-making as choreographic. Singers hear their voices resonating and echoing through unfamiliar architecture, put into contact with foreign spaces buried beneath, behind, and within their own backyards. They hear their voices accompanying performance traditions from across the globe but embedded across the alleyway. Each spot is site-specific, connected to the particular local corner and surrounding structures, yet global too, bringing Tehran, Tokyo, and Londrina together in implausible collisions.

Since the 1990s, many critics who consider theatre through postcolonial lenses have regarded transcultural and intercultural approaches to performance with scepticism. From Grotowski and Peter Brook to Barba and Ariane Mnouchkine, European directors in the late twentieth century have been accused of appropriating Asian, African, and other forms in ways that participate in cultural imperialism. Many critics, perhaps most notably Rustom Bharucha, have criticised intercultural theatre's tendency to appropriate 'oriental' signs to sustain western narratives and subjectivity, mythologizing and decontextualizing Asian forms.[6] When it comes to a sacred text like the *Mahabharata* or an old tradition like Kathakali, western incorporations of these systems of meaning can manifest like tokens of exotic souvenirs long associated with performances of empire: something stolen, ripped from context, used superficially to serve the highly individualistic vision of a western auteur. Even when artists from many backgrounds work together, the leadership of a European director or financial support of a western institution can make it so that the cultural exchanges are never equally valued. The exchanges between cultures, the argument goes, are framed as a European marketplace, just one that exhibits global imports. Even when barters and intercultural collaborations happen on Asian or African soil, the discourse that validates them often presumes a western matrix of values.

Intercultural theatre is fraught not only because European values have through colonialism and so on historically asserted primacy or preference, putting 'primitive' human specimens abducted from other cultures on display for 'civilized' spectators—or condescendingly appropriating Asian theatre forms, as in Puccini's *Madama Butterfly*, to stand in for tragic femininity. Overt condescension is of course still present in popular stereotypes on television, film, and theatre. Perhaps the more insidious dimension of European theatrical attitudes towards the 'Orient' derives from an (admittedly naive) idealization of Asian forms. Artaud and Brecht, paving the way for directors such as Brook, Barba, and Mnouchkine, drew from performance traditions from China and Bali precisely because they found something wanting in the emotionally driven, text-dominated, and largely illusionistic stages of commercial and experimental theatre in the 'Occident.' But as Said elaborates in *Orientalism*, even quite positively inflected western idealizations of the 'Orient' can exoticize and other it, mining apparent strangeness in ways that reify western subjectivity—at the cost of giving voice to specific, contextual, and constantly changing cultures that developed independently of European interests in them.[7] The Beijing Opera (*jingju*) actor Mei Lan Fang, about whose exhibition Brecht wrote his influential essay 'Alienation Effects in Chinese Acting,' did not view his own technique as one of stepping back, with defamiliarizing distance, from the character he played—even though, as a *dan* actor, he specialized in playing female roles through highly stylized movements. Rather, Mei saw his imaginative commitment to really seeing a fictional flower, for instance, as fundamental to his art. Missing (or ignoring) this dimension of Mei's work, Brecht took his reading of the actor's apparent separation from character as offering a 'transportable technique' that actors could use in western theatre. But Epic Theatre's *verfremdungsaffekt* was something traditional *jingju* actors would hardly recognize as rooted in their tradition.[8] Artaud offered a similarly productive misreading after watching an exposition performance by Balinese dancers, allowing him to see *metaphysics-in-action* that directly and hieroglyphically touched spiritual reality rather than the highly codified system of movement embedded in Balinese conventions he simply could not recognize as conventional.[9] Brook's attempts to discover in the actor something transcultural—beneath the mask of all cultures, 'universally' human—can end up looking a lot like a heterosexual European man, the 'norm' of the neutral walk or mask, even as he focuses on the 'essence' of a Noh actor's walk or ancient Vedic myth. Even Barba's International School of Theatre Anthropology, with its beautifully open meetings between cultures, guided by invited masters from diverse traditions, can appear like an intercultural marketplace of ideas dominated by the Europeans who do the buying and selling.

Removed from its home soil, is a tradition replanted in a European garden not decontextualized, appropriated, colonized? Teatro Potlach is vulnerable to similar criticism. Di Buduo often asks collaborating groups from Asian countries to perform their differences in ways that may risk exoticizing them. Festivals and commemorative events often provide official funding for *Invisible Cities* performances, as do institutions, from local, national, and European governmental cultural entities to banks. When the group performs, in Italy or abroad, it sometimes frames the utopian intercultural sensibilities of *Invisible Cities* within popular myths of the host culture, many of which may advance conservative hierarchies, reactionary, authoritarian, or neoliberal interests, or reify corrupt power. Not only do funding sources create circumstances that may proscribe critique; some institutions that support Teatro Potlach's intercultural work oppose immigration, refugee resettlement, internationalism, and so on. In this sense, the participation of performers from Asia, South America, and the Middle East can appear a cynically hollow display of cosmopolitanism, or outright orientalism, that remains comfortably entrenched in powerful interests rooted in nationalism and xenophobia. Taken strictly as political discourse that operates within ideological and institutional frameworks, the intercultural work of Teatro Potlach, like Odin Teatret, may seem to extend imperialist modes of interaction with nonwestern performance practices.

This ideological critique of intercultural theatre, however, would fail to integrate a crucial dimension of Teatro Potlach's work: its organic growth through sincere relationships. The same is true for Odin; at least it was part of its initial contact with other cultures. Barba, long an immigrant himself, did not reach for Kathakali like a costume piece because he thought it would operate well on the level of categories and signs. His exchanges began rather through meeting and then working with, learning from, specific individual performers from India. Similarly, Di Buduo and the other members of Teatro Potlach have gradually developed working friendships, through festival invitations, through their travels, through chance encounters and introductions. Over time, the group's connections to other places have deepened and grown, more closely resembling organic processes of mutual influence than orientalist collecting practices.

In the garden of Teatro Potlach grows a cherry tree from Denmark, a gift from Odin Teatret. The soil surrounding is Italian, Sabine, and yet the tree's roots are deep here. The tree is an echo of its Danish ancestors, but that does not mean it cannot make its home here, drawing from this land its particular nutrients and from these skies the rain that plumps the fruits and feeds the artists. The actors and technicians who have been here for a while—40 years or more—and those who have been here only a few days pause between sessions, between workshops, to be together and eat the cherries. These cherries are a gift from one theatre to another, and from one place to another. To ask if they are Danish or Italian is to confuse their deepest connections to place with national labels that do not represent anything essential about the lands they name. Much more importantly, people gather in the courtyard to eat them at wooden tables, on benches or standing. They share fruit, practice scenes, demonstrate techniques from their disparate lineages, or tell stories of their hometowns. From over a dozen countries and nearly as many theatrical traditions, no one seems to perform a mere souvenir that superficially represents a category of people (nation, city); they bring their backgrounds, their homes, with them in intimate details and essential energies. One night a few summers ago, a conversation between a Balinese dancer, Kamigata-mai performer, and Italian actor shared where their traditions place the centre of gravity: in the shoulders, the pelvis, the head. These three spoke of balance, tension, mutual concerns but from disparate journeys, long into the night.

In the lead-up to 2017's Fara in Sabina *Invisible Cities*, festival participants brought their home cities with them in photographs, videos, and brief physical scores combined with words or songs they carried. Di Buduo asked participants to bring images of their bedrooms, kitchens, and footage of streets in their home cities. Sharing these images and propositions, each participant had the chance to see quite literally where everyone else was coming from. As he developed the path for *Invisible Cities* a few days later, Di Buduo wove into the route through town deep intersections between different cities (Rio de Janeiro, Tehran, Palermo, and so on): a wedding custom from this city, a funeral song from that one. These intersections did not so much represent a greater message about globalism or site-specificity or cultural exchange. Rather they supported each other in a gesture of life: they radiated outwards into a new world, a new kind of global city, formed not by radical antagonism to the past, positioned against local customs or personal roots, but instead by the interwoven threads of their disparate travels and the memory of Fara in Sabina. The attentive spectator-traveller can notice something subtle walking through town during *Invisible Cities*: these intersections appear at the very essence of any city. What is a city but a created world made of differences put into contact, of different people's journeys and memories and subjective experiences? The people of the city overlap, intersect, grow into something rich and interwoven—not despite but because of their diversity.

Notes

1 Ian Watson, 'Invisible Cities: an Interview with Pino Di Buduo,' *Negotiating Cultures: Eugenio Barba and the Intercultural Debate* (Manchester University Press, 2002), 166.
2 Qtd. in Watson, 23.
3 Eugenio Barba, *The Paper Canoe* (Routledge, 1995), 105.
4 Ibid., 47.
5 See Marcel Mauss, *The Gift: The Form and Reason for Exchange in Archaic Societies* (Routledge, 2002) and Georges Bataille, *The Accursed Share*, vol. 1 (Zone Books, 1988).

6 See Rustom Bharucha, *Theatre and the World: Performance and the Politics of Culture* (Routledge, 1993).
7 Edward Said, *Orientalism: Western Conceptions of the Orient* (Penguin, 1995).
8 Min Tian, '"Alienation-Effect" for Whom? Brecht's (Mis)interpretation of the Classical Chinese Theatre', *Asian Theatre Journal* (1997), 200–22.
9 Tsu-Chung Su, 'The Occidental Theatre and Its Other: The Use and Abuse of the Oriental Theatre in Antonin Artaud', *NTU Studies in Language and Literature* 22 (December 2009), 1–30.

13
CITIES AND EMPIRE
London

Ah, London: *The* City. You dwarf other cities in sheer *citiness*: bustle and productivity and reinvention, literature and performance, riches and slums. You surpass them in your global influence and affluence, your imperial sins, your souvenirs pillaged from other cities displayed in public museums and private collections. Your ill-gotten loot is the finest in the world.

You are London, the City who makes New York look utilitarian and Johnny-come-lately, who makes Rome seem a relic of the ancient world, a ruin. Compared to you, Caracas is too hot and Oslo too cold; Paris too pretentious, Houston not pretentious enough; Tokyo too fast, New Orleans real slow; you make Singapore look too clean and Mumbai polluted; Seoul technocratic, Baghdad Luddite; Berlin perverse, Boston priggish. You are the Mean Time against which every other time zone appears fast or slow.

You, London, will always be young, sprouting great gherkins of glass and London Eye, but have always already grown old: stone, ivy, fog pouring thick through Whitechapel alleyways haunted by Jack the Ripper. Defeated, burned to the ground, bombed to rubble, you were born again in new political regimes or publishing houses and banking firms, reborn too in cool gardens, the grey dignity of parliament, and electric life of Mayfair. You stretch through circuitous streets towards the Old Truman Brewery in the east where the young gather to make live art all night and pick through handmade jewellery and pashminas the next morning, where Tube drivers need therapy to deal with all those suicides on the tracks, where Bangladeshi curries spice the air. You, City, reach up too, in glass skyscrapers, repurposed cathedrals or factories, great gleaming sculptures to human ambition. Your invention and lively displays carry residents and travellers to a model of global civilization. You transcend any specific city, yet this very transcendence makes for a distinctive urban identity.

You, London, are not of England, which is smaller than you, quainter, better suited to sheep. You are not just an international city. You are the Capital of the World. In the rebuilt Globe, the groundlings are from everywhere—just as, inverted, Shakespeare's plays travel everywhere these travellers are from, adapted into a hundred languages, a thousand ethnic milieus. Directors from Johannesburg to Calcutta have since the 1960s brought their adaptations of *The Tempest* and *Twelfth Night* back to stages like those of the National Theatre, in part to show the city its influence, the diversity of its legacy. Some of this diversity has even clapped back at its English source, told off London's colonial soul with stage designs of islands where slavery, cultural conquest, and ecological harm indict the culture that caused them from a distance.

Your sooty smokestacks and gin-soaked tenements once exemplified capitalism's worst abuses even as your libraries nurtured its fiercest critics. Marx's body is buried beneath you, you who showed him the mechanisms of production and ideology. You showed him capitalism's guts in the operating theatre of your streets, through the bloody suffering in your factories—but also in books of history and economics. Your capitalism has intertwined with empire, drawing tea and chutney to the Thames along with a vast array of ideas and immigrants. Your global pillaging, sunset-less at its height, built the museums and universities that designed the modern world. Your Great Exhibition of the Works of Industry of All Nations displayed massive machines as well as human specimens where Darwin and Dickens, the Brontës, George Eliot, William Wells Brown, and Lewis Carroll could observe the conquered peoples of the world displayed in reconstructed native habitats. Writers bore witness to this human zoo in words that crossed the world.

You, London, are the city of citations: where every publisher publishes. Where else? London could be made of words. From the diary of Samuel Pepys to the novels of Zadie Smith, London unfolds in words and phrases, and they unfold in London. Woolf's Mrs. Dalloway walks through shops and thinks forward and back in time, in twisting recursive sentences; her daughter sees the city from the top of a serpentine bus, her view of things interwoven with memories and anticipations. I think their thoughts, I walk their steps when I walk in London. Their literariness saturates what they see; they write the city into being. A royal car drives by, leaving 'a slight ripple' that flows 'through glove shops and hat shops and tailors' shops on both sides of Bond Street': a ripple of attention, a ripple of common associations, thoughts 'of the dead; of the flag; of Empire.'[1] I walk down Bond Street nearly a century later; there is no such ripple. No thoughts of the dead, not those dead anyway; they are too long dead to occupy us now. So is the Empire, though its legacy lingers modestly, in gilded lion statues and Indian restaurants and Australians who never returned from gap years and now run youth hostels. There is no such ripple on Bond Street today, but I see how there could be; I imagine there is. Other travellers carry Woolf's words too, so we might share this imagined ripple. In the novel, a plane sky-writing overhead attracts the attention of pedestrians who stop in their tracks, who try to read its seemingly significant message. The people in the novel look up; they dwell for a moment of reading together, of seeking in the 'thick ruffled bar of white smoke which curled and wreathed upon the sky in letters' some prophecy, or war news, or meaningfulness of any sort.

Alas, no, just an advertisement for toffee. Alas, modernity. Collective attention is gathered by cars and planes, then dispersed, fractured back into a million pieces. But even fragmented and separated, Londoners walk on throughout the novel, on a single day at the end of the empire, united by hourly bells. Peter Walsh, away many years in India, walks along familiar London streets; he overlays what he recalls, what he yearns for, on the teeming masses, casting pedestrians pursuing their daily concerns into his private romantic desires. He makes up stories about others, as we all do, in all cities, though London more than most is made of these projected stories; it is the great stage whose little stages microcosmically reproduce its intricate immersive performances. London is the city where an actor playing Jacques first spoke Shakespeare's words 'All the World's a Stage'; it is the city where such an insight was most obvious.[2]

★★★

London, I always came to you for theatre. The first time you were my introduction to Europe. My fellow traveller and I were just two graduate students travelling with a purpose, Heathrow the theatre lobby to a two-month Grand Tour between important theatre cities: London, Paris, Berlin, Amsterdam, Krakow, Prague. (Reader, I married that woman.) The ostensible purpose of that trip was a few weeks of intensive study in Poland with Gardzienice, a post-Grotowskian theatre group in the woods near a mostly agricultural village, but, in my memory, it has always seemed baked in to the theatricality of European travel that London is its gateway, its lobby. This framework makes it hard for me, like so many travellers, to grasp the U.K.'s struggles to sever its economic and cultural continuity with Europe—a decision favoured by the national Brexit vote but naturally loathed in London, the World City.

All my visits to London have been for theatre, mostly as a graduate teaching assistant for a Shakespeare seminar in Oxford. Evenings were sometimes in Stratford but mostly in London, for the National, the Old Vic, the Menier Chocolate Factory. Every trip surrounded a performance, if not of Shakespeare then of Churchill or Shaw. As soon as we arrived in the chartered bus, the students' attention exploded: the curtains opened and the world lit up. They were immersed in dynamic webs of South Asian, West African, and Eastern European culture infused with financial investment made possible through global commerce and power. Together we saw international plays and intercultural adaptations, exhilarated at the crossroads of civilizations.

★★★

I feel exhilarated even amidst traffic, here outside the Nando's on South Lambeth Road, though overwhelmed and anxious too, wary of the swirl of cars and coaches. This busy intersection was once part of nearby Vauxhall Gardens—a pleasure garden in Kennington where people once sought relaxed entertainments among the manicured bushes and trees, attended outdoor theatre, listened to music while strolling, and generally relished the sensory experience of the outdoors. The gardens wove the natural world into the fabric of the city and its cultural life. In *Performance, Transport and Mobility*, Fiona Wilkie describes how Anna Best and Paul Whitty's 2004 protest performance *Vauxhall Pleasure* staged a choir of 50 singers here, where they sang to the passing cars; their presence invited spectators 'to pick out the singing voices from the relentless traffic hum' and reminded them of the site's now bulldozed history, the road's subsequent air pollution levels, and its inhospitable evolution from a pedestrian's perspective.[3] Like so much of you, London, this busy intersection is haunted by what it once was, a Hamlet's Ghost who arrives in spooky apparitions to insist on returns of the repressed and revenge for the oppressed. No retribution for neoliberal development is possible, though; the city must move on; performance will have to do.

But the future is open, and you, London, beckon your global citizens to dream it. During the summer of 2017, the London Museum exhibited an interactive installation called *My Point Forward* by the performance group Blast Theory—whose *Rider Spoke* engaged London's streets through geolocation, recorded memories, and bicycling through the city. The website for *My Point Forward* describes the installation:

> As you enter the exhibition space, a large projection screen is in the centre of the room. On it, a silent film is playing. The film shows a place in the city from a single vantage point. As you move closer, you hear a voice talking about the future in this place. Then a second voice shares their thoughts about the same place.[4]

Behind the screen, the spectator eventually discovers, is a secret 'placeless' place, a darkened room where you enter the chorus of voices, where you add yours. Video prompts invite you to say what you would create here. Can you speak the invisible city into being? Could this collective exercise in imagining the city from a particular spot extrapolate it collaboratively, democratically into a possible future?

You, London, are not the sum of your possibilities nor the measure of your pasts, but the interwoven imaginations of those who have reimagined you in theatrical visions, from Inigo Jones to Blast Theory. Your doorways lead to other doorways, which lead to book covers, or proscenium curtains, or memories of empires at sunset.

Notes

1 Virginia Woolf, *Selected Works of Virginia Woolf* (Wordsworth, 2005), 138.
2 Dora Thornton and Jonathan Bate, *Shakespeare: Staging the World* (British Museum Press, 2012).
3 Fiona Wilkie, *Performance, Transport and Mobility: Making Passage* (Palgrave, 2014), 86.
4 See www.blasttheory.co.uk/projects/my-point-forward/.

14

CITIES AND DESIRE

Singapore

The city meets the traveller (of sufficient means) with glass shopping malls, high-rise condominiums, thousands of teas and curries and sea creatures for sale, air-conditioned tunnels running beneath and between tall buildings. Desires for tropical flowers, entertainment, performance, massages, and food here are proscribed within definite limits, neatly packaged consumer exchanges under the watchful authority of the city state. A wide variety of cuisines proliferates in Singapore, and travellers of course try what they can: chicken rice and crab at hawker stalls, delicate oolong from a Chinese tea shop, the malodorous durian fruit. But all this culinary theatre is framed within a social system that does its best to sanitize and appropriate the tropical jungle and sea out of which it emerges.

The people and their customs draw vitality from the ancient confluence of three streams: Chinese, Malay, and Indian. Modern Singapore was forged through the violence and commercial forces of empire too: English colonization in the nineteenth century and Japanese occupation during the Second World War. The capitalist but autocratic republic of today blends explosive development with authoritarian control, enforcing a regularity that keeps sanctioned culture within definite boundaries; it also keeps the economy humming. Spitting or spray-painting foreigners are caned. The streets are free of cigarettes and chewing gum. Experimental performance that plays with subversive sexual and political ideas is censored—but then that censorship can often become a crucial step towards local and international recognition. In underground drag bars, queer performance artists poke at the limits of the law. In courtyard cafes overgrown with tropical flora, Balinese dancers move ritually and trancelike for hours into the hot night. The apparatus of the state goes on, ruthlessly efficient, outside these enclaves. The local economy—bars, cafes, hookah places—flourishes at the edges of these performances.

Couched deep between concrete apartment towers there is a neighbourhood continuous with Singapore's more distant pasts: Little India. In Spell#7's 2004 immersive walking performance *Desire Paths*, spectators took a trip through this neighbourhood while listening to headphones connected to a Walkman. I took a taxi with my fellow traveller to get there. It was ridiculously inexpensive at the current exchange rate against our U.S. dollars, so taxis became our main passage through the island nation over the course of the week or so there. This blend of mobility and passivity, shifting between scenes in the back of a small cab, made our small encounter with Singapore feel cinematic. But the city's pasts, so paved over here, sprouted defiantly through cracks in the sidewalk, causing ripples in the smooth screen.

Out of the cab and into the streets: past crowded spice shops, beneath a brightly coloured cow sculpture peering atop the Hindu temple, to 65 Kerbau Road. We received our Walkmans at a counter. I pressed play, staggering my start time with my fellow traveller in order to remain alone, experiencing what she experienced but a few minutes afterwards, a few metres behind. The text by Ben Slater and Kaylene Tan instructed me when to turn, often where to look, although I directed my attention within a world notably vaster and full of other possible choices. It was not that the words determined my steps and gaze, but they haunted my way through the neighbourhood. The recorded, carefully crafted dramaturgy felt intimate yet far away, detailing these streets' pasts: here the one-time race track, there the site of terrible bombing during the war. Evan Tan's layered sound design brought these atmospheres into a startling presence, uncanny to hear as the streets flowed along with the life of the present day: people riding motorbikes over former fields of the dead. Recorded footsteps, a constant rhythm in the background, regulated the spectator-traveller's gait—roughly bringing me to the next turn in the journey at the appropriate moment. The juxtaposition between what I heard and saw felt both immersive and cinematic. Spell#7's advertising emphasized the perceptual immersion of the journey:

> Listen to the sounds, the stories, the noise, the whispers, the secrets, follow the orders, get lost, be found, investigate further, check the map, drink some water, keep your eyes peeled...Two narrators compete for your attention: ghosts or lovers, they have gone down this route many times before and this time they implore you to follow.[1]

These voices joined the dead, their recorded presence constantly reminding me that they were no longer here, that I was walking in their steps. Speaking of their longing journeys over the years, chasing and missing each other through alleyways of Little India, their voices made me feel somewhat achingly my relationship to others who walked this route. I followed in the steps of my fellow traveller who walked before me. And the steps of those other travellers who had walked *Desire Paths* before her, and of those who travelled here before the members of Spell#7 ever thought of the piece. And the steps of the people who walked these paths over all the millennia before Singapore was a word. The origin of the performance's name comes from the 'desire paths' created by walkers' chosen routes worn over the years into the earth. Paved roads sometimes follow these paths, growing organically from the layers of journeys that have taken place here, from the layers of people who have travelled through and created this space. Here, beneath the official history and name: the traces of previous journeys, anonymously blended into each other.

Elements of the performance's dramaturgy emphasized the future too. Not only would walkers come after me, repeating many of my exact steps and gestures. More arresting and surreal was the parrot who read fortunes. Apparently people have been coming to this parrot for a while. After asked, the parrot chooses a card upon which the interested customer can read a vaguely phrased fate. I wish I could remember my fortune now, but I do recall that as the recorded voice from the past directed me to ask this parrot in the present to tell me what to expect in the future, I felt suspended in a mysterious temporal state. I was both a small accident of history blown along by forces beyond my understanding and a traveller standing at the nexus of time, at the centre of the intersection between what has been, is, and will be. As I later drank chai, as directed, in the little cafe, I thought of the other travellers whose hot afternoons were spent here, strangely cooled by the hot tea. I shared in a small way their invisible, spectral presence, along with ghosts of future chai-drinkers I would never meet.

The steel, concrete, glass city outside Little India brings the traveller jarringly back into hypermodernity. The impressive architecture along the bay frames a particularly totalizing perspective on the city and state's relationship to its geographical, ecological existence as an island surrounded by water. During the annual National Day Parade, Paul Rae notes, 'Singaporeans celebrate their nation's achievements by staging the city'—and in a particularly totalitarian way that makes the natural world part of the city's power:

> With advanced military technology and organizational capabilities at their disposal, the Parade's creators can integrate sea, sky and the surrounding architecture into the dramaturgy, reconfiguring the Bay as a massive stage set, with the Float as an apron at the front. By contrast with the monumental spectacle of the unadorned Bay, and with the over-eager attempts at self-representation one encounters at ground level, this multimedia, multi-vector mass performance felt appropriate to the site, momentarily capable of bridging the human and the mega scale.[2]

Here nature is not so much repressed or conquered as appropriated, made iconic, used to lionize the city state. As Rae details elsewhere, lions are emblematic figures in Singapore: *Singa Pura*, 'Lion City'; they are feline embodiments of nationalist mythology. In giant spectacles and appropriated Chinese lion dances, Singapore performs its ethnic roots blended with radical cosmopolitanism. Singapore stages the relationship between the city and the sea in a way that roars proudly, insisting on its right to mix unlike things: tropical nature and advanced technology, city and state, China, India, and Malaysia, authoritarianism and capitalism. Without natural resources, long subject to foreign rule, Singapore's assured self-staging seems ready to swallow the world.

Notes

1 See www.spell7performance.org/desirepaths.
2 Paul Rae, 'Performing Singapore: City/State', *Performing Cities*, ed. Nicolas Whybrow (Palgrave, 2014), 193–4.

15
INVISIBLE CITIES 4

Kyle Gillette: How has your work changed after travelling to create this in so many other cities?

Nathalie Mentha: I think it changes in the space. Because you see the space with other eyes, not only with the eyes of the actor. You begin to look in another way at the place, from here to you, not from you to here, not as a colonialist, but another way.

KG: More like a tree, growing.

NM: Yes, this for me is the difference. It's another way to work. I build a place in a courtyard. From this, I create a presence. For [one project my] start was the painter Frida Kahlo. The people who enter just stay—look, look how the courtyard is, see something. Just this. Like if you are part of a picture. And this was really interesting: not to do but create a presence. Wait for the place to give something and you just try to be a part of it, without acting. I start really from the space, and how she is sitting here and waiting, but after five minutes like this, you look: what do I see here, what do I see here? I see I could put a plant here, so I go to find a plant. How can I attract the spectator to enter this? I put a lot of orange on the outside by the street. Just the door of this courtyard was a little bit open, then orange, orange, leading in. It's also always about Calvino, always 'I attract you in to tell you this'. But after they see just a presence. So how as an actor can you create space without telling anything? Just through your attention and presence, your reaction, what you do....

After covered fabric tunnels through crowded corridors (alleyways stuffed with musicians, comedians, installations), the 2017 *Invisible Cities* pathway spilled into the public square up the hill, where Zsofi Gulyas and another aerial acrobat repelling from the bell tower drew travellers' eyes upward. Winged, outrageously high up, they opened the stage's height, sharply contrasting the claustrophobic tunnels and alleyways from before. The mise en scène included the towers and steeples, the pigeons nested in holes in the bricks. The sky above. Down in the piazza, Mentha danced like some dream image, like something out of Fellini, holding a parasol, expanding visual space through her gestures and choreography to the edges of the wide square. Side lighting and a sea of cloth drew her dance into a field of horizontal possibilities, freeing after the tight quarters below, creating a vast plane intersected with the angelic dancers beckoning us to look skywards. Projections out of a 20,000-euro projector with enough intensity to blind a person were mapped onto the old church's architectural outlines and filled the lines in with bold primary colours alternating with images of columns, gods, the church's pagan origins. Families walking saw their shadows projected onto the old sacred wall. Then spectators even saw the moon drawn into performance. Irene Rossi teetered beyond the monastery's castle-like precipice; she leaned forward at the edge of a rock wall, jutting into our line of sight at the end of a taught rope. Her attention and gestures appropriated the bright moon through her presence in that evening vista.

My awareness of particular details within these intimate spaces yawned open, drawing in a vaster swath of the world. It is difficult to convey just how powerfully this movement of my gaze opened my heart, relaxed me, and emptied me of ego, if only briefly. I saw the visible world writ large as something radiant, imminent with meaningfulness even if emptied of stable signs.

Rossi and the moon marked the beginning of the spectator's descent down a long road from the city to the forest, through a park populated at its outskirts by Bawa Iwayan, the Balinese dancer, and Keiin Yoshimura, the Kamigata-mai master

FIGURE 15.1 Irene Rossi in *Invisible Cities* by Teatro Potlach; photo by Sayna Ghaderi

from Japan. There they lurked at the edges of town, ritually dancing within the trees, crying out from traditions that seem so far away from Sabine life. Up we went through a narrow trail where kneeling mourners wept at altars to the dead in Portuguese, candles and skulls populating the grooves in the rock. Regnoli performed near a monument for fallen soldiers. Then down, down, down, through intimate and sacred performances embedded along a path most travellers (and even residents) never see. The journey ended at the beginning of a pedestrian road next to a pizza bar, connecting back to the Caffè Belvedere.

But in a sense the pathway never ended, spilling back into the life of the city. I stepped beyond the path of the performance, back into the flow of citizens enjoying the weekend. They drank Peroni and ate pizza, strolling, sitting on benches, their children riding bicycles, their friends listening to an alt-rock band playing at the bar. The life of the city, seemingly oblivious to the journey spectators just took above, continued that journey, connecting the end to the beginning, creating a circle—but also connecting seamlessly to the aesthetic intensity woven through town by Teatro Potlach's project. Here we were: travellers, residents, artists mingling and blending into the fabric of the nightlife. Here we were, paying attention to the strangers that we passed with fresh eyes ready to take them all in. Here, still warmed by the aftereffects of *Invisible Cities*, we recognized life, a world too often obscured by urban pressures but capable of emerging like a flower growing obstinately through a crack in the brick road.

★★★

At the end of *Invisible Cities*, Calvino writes that Kublai Khan's atlas contains not only cities within the empire but also possible cities, future cities. Marco Polo can glimpse these future cities at times, through 'an opening in the midst of an incongruous landscape, a glint of lights in fog, the dialogue of two passersby meeting in the crowd.' The traveller sees through his travels—in the liminal states between cities, between scenes—a composite utopia he would perform into being: 'I will put together, piece by piece, the perfect city, made of fragments mixed with the rest, of instants separated by intervals, of signals one sends out, not knowing who receives them.' Within the fabric of the imperfect, even hellish cities he has known, he has seen glimpses of the invisible city. This city, like Plato's *Republic* or Augustine's *City of God*, does not exist except as a notion, a rumour, a glimmer, a moment of hope: 'the city toward which my journey tends is discontinuous in space and time, now scattered, now more condensed.'[1] Its existence only comes into being through the search for it, and it is a city whose geography is never fixed.

But the city is cruel to utopia ('no place'). Brutal injustice and totalitarian regimes choke the life out of cities from Aleppo to Hong Kong. What is the point, Khan asks, of utopian dreams when the whole world is going to hell? Khan's empire was crumbling, his cities burning with iniquity and suffering, his dynasty soon to be dead. But Polo replies that this apocalyptic thinking is misguided. The inferno is already here, 'where we live every day, that we form by being together.' In order not to suffer it, one must either 'accept the inferno and become such a part of it that you can no longer see it'—become a highly trained businessperson or warrior or propagandist, say—or do something much harder and more special. The second choice 'is risky and demands constant vigilance and apprehension: seek and learn to recognize who and what, in the midst of the inferno, are not inferno, then make them endure, give them space.'[2]

This is the work of *Invisible Cities*, of Calvino and Teatro Potlach, of the traveller, of the artist. It is the work of anyone who wants to see and protect who and what are not inferno. This work is not connected to production, accomplishment, power, triumph, sophistication, or virtue. It involves rather a total act of care: of seeing in the visible what is not visible, its latent possibilities. It involves giving yourself up to the task of attending to the world. It involves performing the dreamed of city through the streets of the mortal city.

Notes

1 Italo Calvino, *Invisible Cities*, trans. William Weaver (Harcourt Brace Jovanovich, 1974), 126.
2 Ibid.

16
DIRECTIONS

Long before Thespis apocryphally emerged from the chorus to perform the western stage's first dramatic character—long before the dithyrambic chorus itself—ages before epic poems commemorating pseudo-mythic monarchs, millennia before Yoruba Egungun masquerades and Egyptian processions for dead pharaohs—an actor was born. Not the first actor ever, but the first actor in this one particular prehistoric community. Perhaps other actors were born the same way. Too little reliable evidence remains.

It happened like this, or so the story goes. A gathering of people formed a community. In this way, the gathering was already on its way to becoming a small city, though it remained relatively nomadic, following patterns of seasonal abundance in the forest and the migration of prey. People went away to hunt and gather but returned to the group, shared everything in common. Group members stuck together to share tasks and divide labour, and then to pick up and move along when elders determined it was time. As a result of changing climate conditions, and eventually through the advent of agriculture, the gathering began to dwell reliably in one place. Their gathering became a geographically proscribed way of life, a village. Group members travelled less and less, yet the urge persisted too—villagers yearned to travel but only dared to do so in the stories they told about the past and the worlds they visited in dreams. Rather, they built and dwelled, proscribing their routes into repeatable patterns.

One day, after many generations, moved both by stories about the past and her dreams, a villager travelled beyond the hills, far past where any villager had travelled before. The traveller eventually came across a city (some anthropologists insist this was the ancient city Uruk, though many scholars question the evidence supporting that rumour, sourcing it to a single fourteenth-century psychic in Alexandria). What the traveller saw in the city was both familiar and strange: recognizable as another village like her own but one magnified many times, multiplied in population and architecture, with diverse patterns of relation, inscrutable signs to indicate food, love, or danger, abstracted relations to the land, strange rituals to summon invisible forces or prevent a local god's wrath. Here, ideas developed richly as people lived in large buildings like beehives, intersecting in constantly accelerating networks of conversation, storytelling, images, commerce, and cultural exchange, from restaurants and markets to courts and performance venues. Divisions of labour produced efficiencies and specialties, developing rich webs of culture. At the same time, the work and its harms became poorly distributed, and distributed primarily to the poor. In fact, the city multiplied and worsened poverty, allowing some to lack basic needs even when plenty of food, energy, and shelter existed for everyone.

The differences between the city's way of life, its stone architecture and sophisticated people, its weird economics and performance cultures, showed the traveller something interesting about her own village by contrast. The city demonstrated vast possibility, including what a village like hers could become over time as it develops into the future. This was simultaneously a utopian and dystopian thought, for there were great wonders and horrors she saw in the city. The traveller recognized in that foreign place things those city dwellers could not see. They could not see their own urban ways as remarkable, just as she never had seen her village as remarkable. Their way of life was simply how things had always been done, as far as they knew. Except for the prophets and philosophers, most of the city's population went along without seeing what, in its life, was odd or worth commenting on. But the traveller was like a spectator seeing her first big spectacle. She showed citizens through her openness, her response, her encounter with the city what it was like for an outsider: extraordinary in beauty and technological possibilities, horrible in plague, poverty, and exploitation. Through the presence of the traveller, whose attention and movements awoke citizens to their city with fresh eyes, they saw the invisible cities that had been repressed by layers of habit and history.

When the traveller returned to her own village, she was possessed with an energy, an urge to share what she had experienced. But she struggled to convey what she had seen in the strange city beyond the hills. She tried to describe it in words, but her fellow villagers could not picture the foreign city, for they had no points of reference. She tried to visualize the city in figures drawn in the sand or on rock walls, but her fellow villagers could not feel what it was like to be there. So she recreated, through the memory of her body, the experience of travelling along those foreign paths. She experienced for a second time, through the work of her imagination and expressive faculties, what it was like to encounter people with foreign tongues, foreign rituals, foreign ways of growing or gathering or preparing food. She adapted this foreignness to what she knew of her fellow villagers, their popular idioms and familiar gestural vocabularies. Like a shaman mediating between the living and the dead, she became a bridge between places. Like a medium, she brought the presence of the city into the centre of the village.

What emerged in front of the spectators (who only now became spectators for the first time) was something they had never witnessed. The traveller's movements were precise and distilled, pregnant with associations. Her voice modulated to capture the way those other people spoke. Her journey within a small space near the fire suggested a much larger journey beyond the hills. Her muscles contracted and her eyes looked up as she created on the flat land what it felt like to walk up an incline. And in those eyes, looking left and right, she saw again that foreign city superimposed onto the space of her own village. The spectators, almost magically, saw it too. They drew from their own memories, including dreams, to fill in images, but in this primordial theatre they were transported. When the performance ended, everyone sat in silence, eyes closed, impressions resonating along their eyelids and through their bodies. As they returned, the next morning, to their everyday reality, citizens saw the magic there too. They saw their village as if for the first time, both in the rich fabric of performance that brings it to life each day and as a site of future possibilities: the invisible city as hopeful promise (and dire warning) about what lies ahead.

The prompts and exercises that follow have evolved over the course of workshops, classes, devising processes, and rehearsals spanning over a dozen years. Participants have ranged from graduate students at Stanford University and undergraduates at Trinity University to international workshop participants at F.L.I.P.T. in Fara in Sabina. If the way the exercises appear on the page sometimes implies that they are fixed, the actual practices from which these notes emerged were rather improvisational, riffing on whatever emerged, undergoing constant revision. Each exercise unfolded from the particularities of the local place and specific participants. Perhaps you will find yourself drawn to an exercise in the following pages that you want to use, either to create an artwork or to lead students to explore some aspect of urban experience as material. Please experiment, adapt, make it your own; mould it to the needs of your particular situation; or, probably better for most of these prompts, take some element as a jumping off point to find your own way.

The following exercises can be performed separately, but I have often found it interesting to scaffold several of them over the course of days, weeks, or months in order to build work. Some exercises, if executed step by step, may result in a text, drawing, series of photographs, video, or performance, although these products should be regarded as side effects of the process. The process is the key: to experience, remember, and imagine in the city what is normally hidden by habit. Many exercises are open-ended, suggesting journeys to nowhere in particular. They may appear unproductive or useless. In fact, uselessness characterizes many of these prompts precisely in order to redirect travellers' attention to those dimensions of urban experience that fall outside utilitarian circuits of commerce, transit, or tourist itineraries. Like the 'Mis-Guides' by the British company Wrights & Sites, whose work ranges from site-specific performances to urban 'drifts' that take spectators through the city, many of these exercises build on the Situationist *dérive*. Guy Debord used this walking practice to detect the invisible psychogeography of urban space, to lead walkers to see its deep underlying unity. For the members of Wrights & Sites, however, there is a crucial difference:

> Against the Situationists' unitary urban utopia we have mytho-geography: a geography of the city that values equally its legends, its official, municipal and tourist histories, its distortions by commerce, mistakes about it, lies and rumours about it, its dark tales of conspiracy, its physics, its uses in fiction. Rather than seeking to collapse these into a finally resolved unitary 'truth' about the city we have delayed or deferred this synthesis, keeping the different elements in motion.[1]

As with the artistic and pedagogical aims of Wrights & Sites, the deepest stakes of the prompts that follow lie not in bringing into being a Platonic city or Augustine's *City of God* or for that matter a Marxist or Situationist utopia that sheds illusions and unifies the city's essence, nor to expose a single truth that unites a city's mysteries.

Rather, engaging in these tasks involves seeking disparate threads of experience and histories that flow through pedestrians' perspectives, through traffic patterns and buried myths, without attempting to resolve paradoxes or gloss differences. The enigmatic character of travel guides our way: towards anomalies, intersections, mysteries, secrets, anecdotes. The city is not an object that can be contained by a single name: it is an always unfolding network of processes, a confluence of streams, marked by layers of history and myth, by invisible cities.

Cities of memory

Participants in the most recent iteration of this workshop, which occupied most of the first three days of the 2019 F.L.I.P.T. in Fara in Sabina, hailed from 16 countries. Several spoke a combination of Portuguese and Italian, Hindi and French, Inuit and Danish, or Farsi and English, but no single language was shared among all. At times, I asked participants to translate for me. The richest and most intimate moments, however, arose when we left words behind and tried to meet at the level of imagined space suggested through concrete gestures or patterns of movement. Like Marco Polo before he learned Kublai Khan's language, I asked participants to throw themselves into imagining as precisely as possible the neighbourhoods and journeys they have known well. They remembered them in fragments, but connected these through spontaneously invented symbols and resourceful interactions with those objects, architecture, and bodies at their disposal. Without language, participants had no choice but to draw from deep wells of physical, embodied memory. Conjuring cities in concrete ways, they recalled with the level of ingenuity, focus, and care necessary to make others see them too. They had to experiment, trying and failing in a wide variety of ways to embody and relive their cities—until they began to break through, guided by a need to share something deeply felt, to bring along fellow travellers. The point was not, of course, to deliver the city's objectively verifiable surface, like a map or documentary film. Using fragments of remembered walks and shapes proscribed by their movements and attention, participants rather had to make vivid proposals and physical scores that would give those watching a visual and aural scaffolding, a canvas upon which to project their own imagined cities.

Cities of memory 1

This exercise is a primer for the traveller's imagination, also a helpful warm-up before other exercises if participants need to ground themselves.

1. Lie on the floor. Remember a place you have lived that significantly helped form you. See yourself in bed there. Feel in your flesh and your breath what it was like to lie in that bed. Remember smells vividly.
2. Sit up. Gradually stand, if you can, slowly opening your eyes. Superimpose your old familiar room on the room in front of you.

3. Move through your room. Notice the objects closest to your bed, those you remember in greatest detail. Handle them, put them back.
4. Move to other parts of the home. See through your younger eyes your kitchen, if there was one. Go through the main room, perhaps the living room. Then to the front door. Open it and leave.
5. Look back at your home. Perhaps you have a few flights of stairs and a block or two to go before you can clearly see the building where you lived this part of your life.
6. Walk through space slowly, trying to remember in the memory of your body what it was like to be on that street so long ago. Be specific and concrete about what you see and where you step, freely filling in gaps with your imagination.
7. Gradually allow your muscle memory of familiar pathways to inhabit your posture, limbs, gait. Walk through this street at different times of day, different ages in life. Get the feel of the neighbourhood in your bones.

Cities of memory 2

Part one

1. Begin at a designated spot—at the entrance to a building if you have one available. If doing this with a group, allow a minute or two so the previous traveller can stay out of your sight and you out of theirs. Travel without speaking. At first, you may decide when to turn left or right at an intersection or to cross the street based on desire or arbitrary games you impose: alternating between turning right and left, for instance. Then the process of decision-making should grow more nuanced, intuitive, and outside the traveller's egotistic seeking or arbitrary rule. Gradually the process of turning down this or that street should become more organic and spontaneous. Eventually you should feel like you are no longer deciding where to go at all. Rather, you are pulled by the city itself, drawn along its corridors.
2. This first journey may include travel for as long as 30 minutes, though 10 minutes will suffice to establish a repeatable route.
3. Return to the beginning after the predetermined time limit ends. Then repeat your journey as precisely as possible. This time pay closer attention to the way the pathway unfolds like a story. What is this story? Not what does it mean, nor what is its moral. What *is* it?
4. Go back to the beginning again. Then repeat the journey again, but this time divide it into 12 units. The divisions should not be arbitrary but organic, connected to shifts in energy or attention.
5. Repeat these units, noting precisely where each begins and ends. Over subsequent trips, subdivide them further, creating a physical score whereby you look at the same window, step the same steps, touch the same wall each time.
6. As you walk, focus attention on three areas: patterns, accidents, and the physical sensations of walking.

7. On patterns: the ways certain architectural features repeat, or pedestrians behave, or vehicles pass each other. How, for example, do the private dwellings seem to relate to public spaces? Where are places of worship or learning in relation to marketplaces? How do windows suggest domestic stages? How do customers behave at cafe tables? How do people greet each other, or avoid each other, or compete? What social customs are visible in the way women and men dress? How does the city present its deep structure?
8. Notice also accidental details: the cat on the rooftop, the crack in the temple wall shaped like a tree, the opera singer practicing on her balcony. Which sights pop out from the patterns, making singular impressions in your memory as against the backdrop of the more mundane?
9. Finally, and most importantly, notice your sensory experience as you feel it in your limbs, muscles, spine, and breath: the way your calves contract walking down stairs, the way your neck feels when you look up to the bell tower, the way your breath quickens or slows as you move. How does the city make you feel at the most literal and concrete level? Where are your muscular resistances? Where does your attention narrow or expand? What choreography does the city streets demand of you through concrete shifts in tension and release?
10. Return to the room where it all began. In silence, write without stopping for 20 minutes. Relate everything you can recall about the patterns you noticed, the accidental details you remember, the physical sensations you experienced.
11. Lie down on the floor. Recall the memory of the journey you just took in careful detail and vivid imagery. Come to your feet. Recreate it in the memory of your body. Separate parts clearly, then splice them together. If performing this exercise with others, you might also take turns performing your journeys in the room. Do not consult with your notes or plan at this stage. There will be time for that. Attempt, through your movements (and any other means you like), to experience again what you experienced walking. Recreate for the spectators (if there are any) the feeling of your body in transit. Transmit the patterns you noticed. Allow the accidental details to surprise, to interrupt, to emerge. It is not important that you convey images that communicate clear meanings or narratives. Do not try to show anything. Rather, you should experience again your journey with the specificity and care that allows those watching to experience it with you.
12. After these performances, discuss what you saw, the mental journeys evoked. Repeat together, trying the journeys at varying speeds and across different spans.

Part two (if the workshop extends more than one day)

1. At the end of the first day's workshop, each group will choose one of Italo Calvino's *Invisible Cities*. In the 2018 and 2019 F.L.I.P.T. workshops, some participants had passages from cities that stressed the memories of youth, that examined traces of the dead, that burned through consumerist desire in the constant waste of throwaway culture.

2. Using words or images from Calvino's text along with the physical score of your walking, create a proposal overnight. At this point you can plan, rehearse, and build your proposition into something repeatable.
3. Choose a place along your pathway to embed your performance. It can be a small, quite localized alcove or a long stairway, a stretch of road, even the space around a cafe table. The space should be located along your pathway but reduced to no more than one-tenth of your original journey. The duration of each proposition should be no longer than five minutes.
4. Rather than viewing the site you choose to perform this as a neutral space wherein you create the rest of the pathway, draw from its particular physical contours, obstacles, and characteristics to shape your movement, your posture, your voice. Even as you condense your journey into a smaller version of itself limited to one place, let the concrete details of the place shape you: your memory as a traveller as well as the memories that leave cryptic traces (well-worn steps, local lore you overheard, the ways you have observed residents using this space). Feel free to speculate irresponsibly. This is not a museum of objectively verifiable facts but a kind of haunting, where memories and experiences can interpenetrate.
5. For the next stage, perform these propositions, either for other participants or passers-by. If there are others, travel between sites, observing each other's work, attending to the city as a place pregnant with other cities, other possibilities.
6. Return to the room where it all began. Close your eyes. In no particular order, when you feel so moved, say 'I remember…' and then relate a small memory from watching these performances. Allow one another's memories to spark your own. Listen to the memories shared; try to experience them as yours. The exercise ends when the memories slow to a trickle and dissipate. Part ways. Walk into the city. Notice what you see.
7. Optional addendum: have multiple travellers teach each other their physical scores. Create montages that intersplice elements for a rich tapestry of the city's walking journeys. Then let these unfold over a long time, ever incorporating new gestures, new engagements with the topography.

Cities of memory 3

For a group of 8–12, ideally gathered from many different parts of the world for a festival or conference. I led this exercise for the 2019 Festival Laboratorio Interculturale di Pratiche Teatrali in Fara in Sabina. Participants hailed from India, Iran, Greenland, Brazil, Spain, Italy, and other countries.

Part one

1. The first part starts with a visualization, something like a guided meditation. Participants lay down and close their eyes while the teacher invites them to recall a city that has once captivated them. Not a city where they grew up, but

a city they know well enough as a traveller, one that once fascinated them, enthralled them, showed them what a city could be. Students recall small, 'invisible' details: the alleyway behind the grocery store, the water pipe that forms an irresistibly perilous bridge across the gulley.
2. Participants should remain precise in their memories, diligently working to recall patterns and odd details. The teacher should prod them to see concretely, to hear and smell and feel too.
3. Gradually, participants adapt different perspectives. How would this city unfold from the perspective of a stray cat? Or a pigeon who alights on streetlights? A rat? A leashed dog on a walk? A police horse?
4. What do you see as you surge through the streets, on the back of a motorbike? From a car?
5. You are a bird, and you lift above the streets, gradually higher and higher. How does the city unfold below?
6. View your city as a god. Not God, neither an ultimate creator nor judge of the universe, but a god, the sort who's got a city dedicated to you, like Athena overlooking Athens.
7. Stay specific. See particular details in the buildings. Watch individual specks of people walk the sidewalks.
8. Wipe the city out. Not violently, just as if a sandcastle returning to the sea.
9. Sculpt a new city out of clay with your hands, one that has never before existed. Give it topography first, smoothing flat bits, gathering up hills. Pay special attention to the river. The river is the lifeblood of the city. Watch creatures interacting in the forest or valley. Watch people in the city. Watch where they go. Watch their patterns of movement. Watch vehicle traffic, trace their routes.
10. Sculpt from earth the buildings, the main square, the temple, the marketplace, the residential districts, the riverside, the landscaped parks, even the haphazard and neglected backstage areas.
11. Get lost in small details; relish your creation.
12. How would you possess this city if you were a deity responsible for its life and well-being? How might you allow or stimulate it to be?
13. Make yourself small, a little resident. See your small self from above.
14. Make a small, personal journey through your carved city, imagining your avatar below.
15. Return to a lying position. Visualize your journey through this carved city from the inside.
16. Create your journey through this city with careful visual, aural, and olfactory detail. See your city from the incarnated eyes of an angel or god taking on mortal flesh to see as people see.
17. In *Wings of Desire*, Wim Wender's beautiful film about Berlin, angels long to be human as they observe people throughout the city. They watch people on the U-Bahn train where they can hear passenger thoughts in little snippets or in the library where hundreds of readers' thoughts harmonize into the very hum of the universe. Be like the angels. See the people go by. Hear their thoughts.

Mingle with the citizens, the chickens, the cats, the children, the foreigners, the barkeepers and all—even as you remain damned to the outside.
18. What is the name of your city? See it from the outside. From above. From below. In what ways do you recognize its traces? Where do aspects of this city diverge from or offer meaningful refractions of your city?
19. Write your city as if you were Marco Polo describing it to Kublai Khan, or Calvino imagining.

Part two (perhaps the following day)

1. Read your city out loud, in small groups. Play with the text, exploring tempos and speeds, until it becomes second nature.
2. Now describe the city to a partner (or a few), but imagine you share no language between you. You must draw from your resources like Marco Polo before he learns Kublai Khan's tongue: gestures, actions, souvenirs, cries. The point is not to force your total image into the minds of your spectators. The point is to provoke them to see, to present them with actions whereby they can see their own cities.
3. Gradually reintroduce words or phrases from the text you wrote, combining them with your emerging physical score.
4. Create from this a repeatable dance: a dance of the invisible city.

Cities of memory 4

Part one

1. Break into groups of five or six.
2. Each group will arrive in a general area around an area of the city.
3. Within your group's general area, find a specific spot and read a bit of travel writing about a city you have visited.
4. Remember your journey concretely as you read.
5. Physically interact with the urban architecture in your spot, just some simple way. You might walk up and down the stairs or along a route you repeat. Or you might rather engage the objects and buildings of the environment. For example, you might sit on the bench, or lean against a wall, or weave between pillars.
6. Repeat your writing until you have made a simple, repeatable path or a simple way of interacting with your site.
7. Imagine along this path, or in place, that you are speaking to a traveller.
8. You are the tour guide, but through this space you are really talking about the city you wrote of, speaking to a single spectator about it.
9. Read your travel writing out loud as you walk or interact with the courtyard until you can say most of it without looking at the page, just looking in the eyes of your imaginary spectator.
10. Your instructor will come by sometimes to listen.

Part two

1. If you are in Group One, go hear about the travels of others. Only one person should listen at a time to each traveller performing.
2. These fellow travellers, the performer and spectator, should make eye contact as much as possible, but the performer might also direct the spectator's attention, pointing, looking, and gesturing around the environment of the courtyard.
3. For one minute this goes on, then a bell rings. If you are in Group One, move on to another performer.
4. The process repeats five times, so that each member makes contact with five others.
5. After this, Group One returns to pick their performances back up, preparing to perform for the other groups.
6. Group Two takes the place of Group One in steps 1–4.
7. Group Three takes the place of Group Two in steps 1–4.
8. Reconvene in separate groups to discuss.
9. Reconvene all together to synthesize.

From here

1. Go to a spot in town and hang out for a while, documenting everything that you experience. Sink into your experience until it stops being about you. You are just there, like the cat or bench, silent witness to the neighbourhood's passing.
2. Every 10 minutes for two hours, remaining in the same spot, take a 20-second video pointed at the same view.
3. Between these videos, spend your time observing with careful attention but soft enough focus to let many things in at once. List everything you observe, notice, overhear, or feel in a notebook. Your thoughts as much as possible should keep returning to the city around you, yourself disappearing into pure transparency. But as your thoughts do stray, notice how the city triggers them. Keep bringing your mind back to the things you see around you, the actions that unfold. Let go of the separation between your experience and yourself. Each 10 minutes, when you stop to take a 20-second video, mark the place below what you have written.
4. Edit a longer video made of the separate 20-second videos stitched together. For the audio track, read the list of things you observed and the thoughts that strayed, timing your reading to go along with the corresponding videos (or, alternatively, you could do an interesting juxtaposition between incongruous audio and video, or create more complex montages).
5. Play this video/audio on a loop, perhaps as a projection on a wall, or as a laptop, television, tablet, or screen embedded in an installation that includes souvenirs gathered from the spot: scraps of debris, small rocks, nothing stolen of value. You

might join this with any number of other artists engaged in the same exercise. A site-specific gallery full of these going on in different spots could be interesting.

Outdoor-indoor

For one person, patiently, in silence. The elusive power of presence in a performer is rooted in imagination, specificity, and care, whether reached through a Stanislavskian actor's concrete objectives or Keiin Yoshimura's slow, disciplined Kamigata-mai steps. To arrive at this state involves combining the playfulness and freedom of childhood with the rigour of serious work. The same might be said for other kinds of artistic practices. Calvino's Marco Polo has this quality, embodying the act of travel as imagining possible cities into existence—while drawing from remembered walks through real streets. His descriptions interplay with Kublai Khan's experience listening to him, with Khan's memories and leadership over a dying empire. Polo's task, through all the resources at his means, is the artist's task: to make invisible worlds present and tangible. The following exercise is one to hone imagination, practicing the careful integration of perception, memory, metaphor, and travel.

1. Take a walk through your neighbourhood. Notice what you normally ignore. Repeat the same course but notice more deeply. Take your time to stop and pay attention to specific spots that catch your eye.
2. Return home. Find a room in your house where you feel especially safe and comfortable.
3. Move through the living room or bedroom or kitchen. Cast each piece of furniture as a building in your neighbourhood. Name them. See those buildings superimposed in miniature on all the items of the room.
4. Live out a quiet Saturday morning among your things, connecting to each as the building it 'is.' Maybe the sofa is your house, the bookcase a high-rise co-op, the table the farmer's market or 7-11 down the street.
5. Treat each place carefully, attending to its specific contours and traces of history within its layers, paying particular attention to windows and doorways. Closely observe the neighbourhood between. Let yourself see familiar neighbours doing familiar things, or to see what might unfold there.
6. Continue crawling along the floor from object to object, letting the course of your morning at home in this room move through this neighbourhood, like you are a giant among small buildings. See your neighbourhood; walk along as if you are strolling to the coffee shop or bakery, or perhaps across ditches to the only place to buy milk and flour.
7. Take another journey, this time at night. The bars invisible by day open up, if there are bars; or the nocturnal creatures come out. See them as they slither between the cars.
8. Stop often to sit and imagine. You might even lie down on the wood floor between the coffee table and lamp. But for you it is the street, the sidewalk, the main square. The rug is a patch of grass. Become the still point; allow the movement around you to emerge, first at the level of cars and buses and people,

then down to the subtlest details: pigeons, bricks out of place, a crumpled falafel wrapper whisked down the road by the wind.
9. Take your notebook or laptop and begin writing. Write of the neighbourhood you see, its stories pouring out its windows and doors. Write perhaps a dozen beginnings to stories, or catch a few snippets of people on their way from place to place. Tell the story of a single trash bin or leaf as it changes throughout the day. Don't stop writing; keep going. No backspace, no cutting, no correcting, pure intuition.
10. Imagine your words weaving in and out of the alleyways and houses that have inhabited your room's objects. As you type your words travel all through town, through the windows, waking people up, whispering in their ears, bubbling in the tea kettles, billowing out the tailpipes, rustling in the wind through the leaves.
11. Describe in your writing how the beginning of this city—or neighbourhood, or family—came to be. You might think of the popular myths residents have about it, that they sell to travellers. You might think of how different historical forces came together with necessity and accident to develop some businesses and infrastructure along a river. You might imagine how a certain family moved to this particular neighbourhood, and how it's changed over generations.
12. Write from different parts of your living room, imagining you are sitting on or in or among the buildings of your neighbourhood.
13. Then go for a walk around your neighbourhood outside, imagining the things you've just written about.
14. Let this stimulate your research, noting details that you've left out but guided by your stories, your words and histories.

Stray trips

The following prompts are open-ended, barely sketched, little more than a direction to face. Some involve photography or video equipment; a reasonably late-model smartphone is more than enough for our purposes. In many ways your phone is ideal, both more transportable and more discreet than bulky equipment. Any number of these might be combined or performed separately.

- Create a photo series Benjamin's ragpicker might create, documenting discarded evidence of urban life.
- Create a photo series of superimposed oppositions: rich and poor neighbourhoods, up and down views, inside and outside views.
- Photograph and caption visible traces of the city's memory: in cracks and worn steps, in fading signs and disused alleyways.
- Create a video from aboard public transportation that documents transitions between neighbourhoods.
- Write in the same spot all day outside your normal contexts. Let what happens in the city make its way into the text.
- Walk through the city for at least four hours, drifting between neighbourhoods, following curiosities you do not consciously choose. When you return home immediately begin writing and do not stop for one hour.

- Watch Alfred Hitchcock's *Vertigo*. Retrace Scottie's steps and especially drives as he follows Madeleine through the streets of San Francisco. First go as him, always seeking her real ghost. Then go as her, aware that you are being followed, that you are being watched. Lure Scottie to the tower at the Mission. Repeat at different paces, on different vehicles. Begin to notice what emerges.
- Create ten time-lapse videos at various places in the city. Edit these together. Create a simple physical action for each image that you develop from each site.
- Find hiding places. Sketch markers of concealment.
- Give a homeless person an irresponsibly large quantity of money. Give your coat too.
- Use urban maps to choreograph a solo dance. Enlarge the map if possible to cover the dance floor.
- Draw your pathway over a 24-hour period based on data from your smartphone GPS. Draw icons for important parts of the day. Use this map to relive your day, revising and repeating.
- Recreate your day's perambulations as choreography in another space.
- Recreate the journey of your day as precisely as possible, filming from your perspective. Later record a soundtrack of you reading texts written based on your memories of the day. Try again but juxtapose with texts from different days.
- Collect a small sack of scraps that catch your eye over the course of an afternoon. These are your prompts.
- Stalk a cat.
- Take a bus in a small group, as if you were there to see Forced Entertainment's *Nights in this City*. Just look.
- Continue the above until you are moved to step off, then find your way back home. Use this journey back as the material for a short book whose pages alternate between recounting the attempt to find your way and illustrations you draw from memory.
- Study the history of one block through every available means and then stage it. No excuses for limited means: it can be done with a single actor, with nothing.
- Record sounds from 18 spots around the city and create a montage or layered soundscape. Use this for material towards an installation, film, performance, or audio piece.
- Gather as many screens as you can and play a different travel video set in city x on each. Leave alone or combine with a dance.
- Find out about a public ritual and investigate its political stakes and buried myths.
- Attend it and read about it, integrating your observations into a story about the place.

Note

1 Wrights & Sites, 'Mis-guiding the City Walker', 2004, www.mis-guide.com.

APPENDIX

Never the same river twice

In the June 2019 *Invisible Cities*, Di Buduo organized the journey around three themes: the river, Raphael's painting *The School of Athens*, and an archaic bronze-age chariot found near Fara in Sabina that predates even the ancient Sabine tribes. These themes grew out of local resonances. The village sits atop a hill near three important rivers, including the Tiber which flows through Rome and out to the sea near Fiumicino. The river is the lifeblood of Rome and the cities throughout the area, though its deep mythic and ecological significance to urban life is rarely felt during daily commutes. Raphael's painting was commissioned by Pope Julius II to cover the wall he looked at from the desk in his papal office. Julius wanted to see representations of western philosophers and theologians, from Heraclitus to Aquinas, while he thought, while he prayed. The resulting painting, a masterful Renaissance employment of the central vanishing point perspective to create the illusion of depth, mixed with philosophical representations of thought. The third theme centred on an important local archaeological discovery: a pre-Sabine war chariot whose invisible presence under these cities reminds me just how deeply previous generations, previous cultures, are buried beneath contemporary everyday life. Three themes, three streams, were to intertwine, converge: the river (ecology), the *School of Athens* (philosophy), the chariot (archaeology).

Each of the participants' initial proposals had some basis in a city they brought with them, rooted in their specific pasts. These experiences from indigenous communities in Greenland to the busy streets of Ahmadabad in the Indian state of Gujarat provided some initial material developed through the three-day workshop I led called Cities of Memory. Participants also researched the streets of Fara in Sabina, trying to remember through their bodies, drawing from sensory experience and travel to craft pieces that integrated this walking with their private cities. Then, as Di Buduo began to develop *Invisible Cities*, each participant used their pieces as the basis for proposals that would respond to one of the three themes (river, painting, or chariot).

The way these themes played out scenographically throughout the city created deep resonances between them. A river of spectators flowed through the streets, LED-lit fabrics creating a liquid-like flow uphill. Projections of water and flowing cloths created a convergence of rivers in a main square. Moving projections of portions of Raphael's painting lit up the monastery and immersed actresses' performances of brief koan-like texts distilling thoughts of some of the represented philosophers: Heraclitus, Zeno, Pythagoras, Socrates, Plato, Aristotle. The museum and nearby video mapping installations juxtaposed images of archaic archaeological objects lurking behind and beneath the buildings.

My fellow traveller Rachel Joseph joined me this year, in part to perform the international premiere of her piece *Antigone in the City* for the festival. She and I both wrote material for the 2019 *Invisible Cities* in Fara in Sabina, collecting and translating literary quotes about rivers, writing poetic-philosophical texts for actors to perform. We also formed a special relationship to the performance itself. Like spectators, we walked through the course, paying attention to the particular pieces as we went, stopping to look as long as we were interested. But we also performed this looking, writing almost constantly in our notebooks. We often spoke this writing aloud as we wrote, influencing each other through overheard phrases. When we arrived at the end of the course, Rachel Joseph and I sat in two chairs under a specially placed blue light. Here we took turns telling each other, and interested spectators, what we experienced as we went, trying to communicate like Marco Polo and Kublai Khan—really imagining the cities we saw, repeating the journey in the realm of words, of anecdote. We paid homage to our late directing professor Carl Weber, who always started feedback by asking simply and literally, 'what did you see?' After each description, each little memory, we asked, 'what did you see?' And then we listened as memories unfolded, interpenetrated, as spectators gradually swelled to a crowd to hear and remember with us. What follows is our unedited transcription from the final performance.

RACHEL

What did I see?

Begin again.
The performers march. They are going on
A Journey.
We watch them—full of
Anticipation for their next
Steps—I am amazed.
We write—fellow traveller
And I—for love
Of this city
Lighting the way.

KYLE

The river begins to flow and all things go
From sixteen far-flung nations
They enter the city, fellow travellers all
To see this little village a new way
Upward the river flows

RACHEL

Candles for the
Silent one.
He hums and
Finds the way.
Sweet pungent incense.
I am struck by
The stranger's gaze—
Even when
The baby cries.
This is part of
The darkness.
We see them
As we pass
Under.

Strange, their—clicking.
Glances—swept along
With the crowd.
Loud stick. The crowd
Flows
Like a river.

The words
I write are still
Also strange.
The words I write
Are still so strange.

KYLE

The sage blesses with fire
Gives blessings before the city street
Ahmedabad here in Fara
The beggar asks for help
Beneath the place where all things flow
This cloth from the land of Gujarat

Namaste, chai chai chai, advertised along
With Bollywood stars

RACHEL

I walk forward
Little girl.
People everywhere
With enjoyment.
A woman with pasta.
She rubs the pasta
On herself in heated despair.

KYLE

Spaghetti goes not only inside her body but on it
She tries to cool herself with noodles
Mangia mangia, and rub

RACHEL

A secret garden
We see
It faintly between
Bodies.

A garden of delight.
And still the pasta
Is rubbed on skin
Throughout hair—on
The cobblestones.
—it is hot.
—It remembers
The water.

And then…

KYLE

Further on, secret garden
Tended pleasurably by Epicurus
From Brazil but here
The residents of Fara are travellers
And the travellers from India and Brazil are residents
Welcoming Sabine people home again

RACHEL

A sound and
A woman in pleasure
Through turning to
Water over a still man.
Rolling over
She flows
As he is stagnant.

Don't rush.
He lifts her
In the riverbed in
The garden
They are alone
And not.

Flag of pride
Displayed on side
Of building becomes
Part of the performance.

KYLE

In the next green garden
Where soft sex happens
Rolling like a river
The man supports her weight
And so she drifts
Spectators watch shyly, such intimacy
They go above and find another point of view
Looking down below the flag fluttering beyond

RACHEL

There is a man
Contorting.
He had in his
Mouth, as
A moustache,
Vines.
He is alone
Blind
Without hope.
Upright he continues
On.

KYLE

In blue river, blind Butoh
Cool but stuffed with straw
See how he moves, such slow suffering
What do the travellers see?

RACHEL

The water stops
And a woman
Cups her breasts.
She is alone too;
Upset in the midst of a crowd
She shows us old photos.

KYLE

Then red, a horror of heat and passion
Ties the woman to her chair
Can she ever be free of desire?
Photographs on fire

RACHEL

I am seeing old
Friends
Meet once again—my
Fellow traveller—
And then,
A demonstration
Of the properties of
Water.

Old friends rush
To be
Together.
A tube full of potential
As a science magician
Explains the secret world.

KYLE

The Sabine traveller looks at my notebook,
Asks if I am curious—and I am
Then we arrive at the experiments with water
Gulf Stream flow reduced within a little aquarium

Science becomes theatre, even as this theatre is a laboratory
Where we see how things might be
The director watches the cities he has shaped
Arranged for spectators to see

RACHEL

Up we go…
At this moment
Water.
A building alone.
Dark tonight,
Empty.
The performance
Of Venus
on the worn wall.
Her beauty
Indisputable.

KYLE

Empty open place behind the square
Where is the lady of lights? She must be fixing
The philosophers up above in the monastery
But here projected is a philosopher already
A preview of things to come
Then Venus appears, goddess, Angel,
From Vatican to Fara in Sabina
I sit with the old man Francesco Bellini
Whose warmth and hospitality has housed me here before
We wait a moment to share the perspective
From stone steps

RACHEL

Shapes in the square.
There she is—
A woman.
She sparkles,
Curtains blow in the
Breeze, and she
Holds onto a tree
As if in the wind
Like the curtain.
Music swells,

A dance ensues, and
There is no rush in
All this space taken
With presence, water.
They are together.
Water and woman.
Do you see?

I do.

What now?
What the child's eyes
See with flowers
In bloom
On her dress.

KYLE

Then I turn the corner and my heart opens
Waters flow over architecture of the piazza
Saturating all in waves and flow
Together again, rivers converge like curtains
At the Theatre of Cascades
Before they arrive to the sea
Rhea Silvia, the mother of Rome
And the river, as the traveller Goethe saw,
Was identical with her reign (and rain)
Amazon goddess of rivers too
her gems shine as she dances
Holding onto tree
(Calvino warns against the crocodiles)
Then again the curtains close
And the proscenium closes
The Theatre of Cascades disappears
As all things do

RACHEL

Continue moving.
Continue
Inside a
Journey
Wherever it may
take you.
Surrounded by
Light
It continues.

Disappearance—
The woman in lights.

KYLE

We flow too, fellow traveller
Behind the scenes, backstage
To the invisible reality beneath the waters
Behind nature, sea, behind theatrical cascades
The real: the city

RACHEL

Where is my journey?
Where will it take
You?
I don't know—but I'll continue.
Behind the curtains
Where a woman
Rests. We
continue as does
A cat.

The mirror woman holds
A photo with her.

KYLE

A cat has become a spectator, seeing in a Persian mirror
An uncatchable creature of light

RACHEL

To the side—now mud coated
She doesn't have anything but
A body.
Pulling
the earth—handprint
shows a trace of her movements.

Continue…

KYLE

Behind the flowing sea a muddy place: dark muck
Between the buildings
She can never be clean again

So naked with what has been
Then the path between cities becomes for me
The most important part

RACHEL

The mirror, again,
Catches the lights.

Do you remember this from before?
I don't know.
He is her reflection.
Do you remember
Reflections?
And she admires
Her own self.
She admires
Although adrift.

KYLE

The woman from Iran asks for us to see
Her sad photograph and mirror
She sees I am not the man she loves
Who has been gone these thirty years
So sorry to disappoint
We go

RACHEL

I now go to the
Songs with wheat
And candles light
The way.
They sing a song
That I seem to
Remember
Somehow.
I remember
from the
other day.

KYLE

The Polish song, here now as there and Ukraine,
Beckons to the riverbanks

These young people weave their wreathes of straw
And, so haloed, think of love
They want to send their candles and wreathes
Down the river (so dry)
So they can discover fellow travellers

RACHEL

I see bodies
Written on as if
A book I will read one day.
Beauty, I write on one arm
And, on another, the sun,
And then descend.

KYLE

Stop Facebook and Instagram
A new kind of post, an old way to make selfies
Written on the skin

RACHEL

A secret—tell me.
It's through
The door.

KYLE

Then the cellar where last night a monster lurked
Is the spider still here in the cool dark? No,
Only my memory—it haunts this secret place
Maybe now it lurks above?

RACHEL

Another world.
I see these
Fragments of a dream.
They entrance
Despite the
Stares
They howl and growl in the wind
A kind of new world reappears
From the old.

KYLE

Outside another kind of monster, three
Who pace about the glacier, growling
A kind of human before there were cities
Only rivers of ice and cries in the night

RACHEL

There is the
Painter.
He shows his
Work on the
Path.
Frames wait to
Hold your image.
I don't know
What I might
See or sketch
Or believe.

KYLE

A painting here, plants in foreground, then river
Beyond trees. This canvas and others shows
Not the trace of work but painters making,
Focused concretely on their materials
One cuts the canvas to make the texture of trees
And near, the teacher of philosophy sings of stars
While they twinkle in the valley below

RACHEL

See a canvas
Next to her
Swelling
Song—I recall from before.
She sees nature
And the city
Is below.

He scratches the
Canvas.
As stars, moths,
Your worlds
Greet us again.

KYLE

In the gates of the monastery
Two lovers of different tongues
Try to share soft songs
Even as the moment must vanish
Such sweet sorrow and they part
She goes; he loses his fellow traveller
And still he sings

RACHEL

A love song.
A woman suspended in
Near distance.

Now you see?
Yes.
Is it love?
Who knows?
It, this budding sweet,
But things often
Vanish—are not
what they appear
at first glance.

KYLE

As before, as always, there is an angel on the wall
This time introducing La Scuola di Atene
Painted by Raffaello Sanzio for Pope Julius II
So he could see within the flat wall of his office
The minds underlying western thought
So he could see Athens inside Rome

RACHEL

There she is! The angel
All lit up.
I wonder if I will
Become one. So one
Day will I become
Like her?
Become an angel?
Yes.
Do you see her?

Yes—she speaks
Of ancient wisdom
Again like the night before
Faintly remembered.

KYLE

Then the sweet garden of tiny lights,
Lovely little flowers floating, fireflies
Caught in jars like galaxies hanging from trees
A vision of heaven
Not glory so bright it blinds
Just the softest twinkling

RACHEL

The fireflies are
All lit up too.
The fireflies are in
A jar—sweet
Scent of flowers as
In an enchanted kingdom
I dreamed of
As a child. Stars
In a jar. Are you asleep?
Yes, quite.

KYLE

The walls of the monastery are moving, breathing
Ancient thoughts animating their solid stones
We follow candles up

RACHEL

Flames light a way.
The walls undulate
Where prayerful
Sorrow may
Live in peace.
I live here
In sorrowful
Peace.

KYLE

Below, the old men of Raffaello's painting flow
Over the woman who speaks of Aristotle and Heraclitus
And the painting inhabits her, over, around and through
Below the monastery she lies, bathed in the paradox
Of Zeno, always arriving halfway to a city she will never reach
The river of philosophy streams through the woman's veins

RACHEL

A woman lies
On the painting.
She touches
The images scrolling past.
Each thought she has so wise.
Though the men
She rolls over and over again
Receive immortality
She will not.

Refracted the building
Breathes once again.
And there is the city
Gazing upon us, another city.

KYLE

The sweet sad song, she loves who she loves
Glad he is hers and she is his, the devastating love
Of Bonnie for Clyde, like that of Desdemona
Now it has become softer than last time
She hurts, so blue, her sorrow making cries
Into song

RACHEL

She speaks—a
Soft voice
Bathed in blue
Like before
The river.
She struggles
Repeating again
This song also
Suddenly is silent. Do you

Remember? Hoarse from repetition
She sings.

KYLE

Through the blue tunnel another philosopher, a woman tends the walls
And finds meaning in Euclidean geometry, Platonic truths
Meditations on time

RACHEL

In the garden
More forms
Become forms.
I see her again,
On this, nature's stage, another
By the door—once in another
World blows like wind on water.

KYLE

Across from her, another woman philosophizes at the church door:
Tomorrow and tomorrow and tomorrow, Shakespeare creeps
In this petty pace until the last syllable of recorded time,
Blows out this brief candle, stages this walking shadow
Who fruts and strets his hour, tells how this tale is told by an idiot
And then is heard no more

RACHEL

Tomorrow,
Yesterday,
Today.
The wise ones
Look on
As she tells
Ancient tales.
And more
Shadow.
Is my being
A shadow?
Who knows.

I walk alone.
These flowers again
Lit up like

Magic. The wind
Through the gate
And there
Is that old
Sorrow
Once again.

KYLE

Outside the gates of heaven is a red hell of suicidal sorrow
Emptied, a man just beyond the reach of the sacred place suffers
How can he face the inferno inside him, which seems to come
From all around?

RACHEL

As if flying—he
Is unhappy.
Am I?
Yes.
Can you help him?
No.
What now?
Recall everything
He feels as your
Own—in this way
I cannot
Breathe or
Quiet such sobbing.

KYLE

Yes yes yes, *si si si*
Torn at the bottom of the hill
The man child's play is ripped by aggression

RACHEL

He is on the hill again.
Running through straw—he's so
Alone too—as am I
Separate from fellow traveller.
Dust rises from
His movements.
I am sure of
Death, but nothing

Else.
Come back to life.

Benches lit up and
Alcoves beckon taking on water
As if a baby river.

KYLE

In the red field on the Persian rug
Another lies in his bathrobe
Speaking on the phone for all to hear

RACHEL

In a cave
He is fallen. Lying there
Robed,
Alone. I am ashamed
That he speaks
So loud.

KYLE

I am free, I see, to think between cities
As I travel and become connected in this village
To stories emerging between the scenes

RACHEL

Juggler—unveiling
Again—old man.
I can see through
Walls can you?
No.
Why?
I haven't juggled for
Many years.

KYLE

And there within the wall
A city before cities
Revealed, juggling
Chariots from long ago

RACHEL

He, on the bench, talks crazy
Although I'm not convinced
That he's not faking it.
His song and cane.
So enter the
Museum.
Enter—again.
Old things.

KYLE

The old man on the bench, outside the ancient Sabine museum
Sings aloud old songs and recalls himself in this city as a young man
Across from the young man who juggles
Each ball revealing more of what came before

RACHEL

Ballet—form—the
Body. Sound
Of mechanical voice
As they bend
And straighten.

Another
Room
By the
Old vase.

Dancers and shadows.
I love the night.
This modern song
As she twists
In old, so old, room
Did you see
It before?
Indeed, I did.
It seems
Right to
Cross paths—
Fellow traveller.

KYLE

The dancers in the museum, slow and graceful
Light against things older than Romans could tell in their histories
And the hip young movement to contemporary dance in the room
That brings the outside in…

RACHEL

Down stairs.
Man running—a
A sign
From God—
Get out
Now
While
There is still a
Chance.

KYLE

Then at last we all descend the steps
To Trastevere: here one actor, one poet
Trilussa, who tells stories that keep people rapt
Such space she shapes with hands and words
Invoking with lightness the heaviness of philosophies
Which she blows away into the night air
So softly

RACHEL

There she is!
She beckons
To spectators.
Sitting, she
Carefully tells
Tales, thoughts,
The world through
Gestures.
I admire
Her.

KYLE

And there, the empty chairs, now bathed in blue
I arrive with you, fellow traveller
And remember the journey together
Let's begin again.
What did you see?

RACHEL

Now I arrive.
I might sit where
I might encounter
Another.
Fellow traveller bathed in light.

Shall we sit to tell
A tale of this
Journey?
Turn pages to the beginning.
I shall.
Fellow traveller follows.
We sigh only to
Begin again.

What did you see?

INDEX

20,000 Leagues Under the Sea 75

Aeschylus 4, 5, 6
Akihiko, Senda 52
anthropology, theatre and 58–59
Antigone in the City 110
apartment dwellers 11–13
art and relationship with reality 59–60
Athens 4–5, 6, 30
Augustine of Hippo, Saint 6–7
authenticity 28–29, 29–30; performance of 41

backstage tours 29–30
Barba, Eugenio 61, 76, 77, 78, 81
'barters' 77–78
Baudelaire, Charles 14–15
Baul, Parvathy 47
Benjamin, Walter 14, 15
Blade Runner 10
Blast Theory 87
Bown, Alfie 11, 13–14
Brecht, Bertolt 76, 80
Buddhism 8

Calvino, Italo: *Invisible Cities* 2, 20–22, 24, 30, 60, 74, 94–95, 101, 106; *Six Memos for the Next Millennium* 78
capitalism 15, 85, 88
Castellucci, Romeo 66
celestial cities 7
Certeau, Michel de 9, 11
Christianity 7
Circus Circus 69

cities of memory workshops 99–106
City Dionysia Festival, Athens 4–5
City of God 6–7
Cole, Teju 19
Coliseum 66–67
Confucianism 8
cultural imperialism 79–81

Dante 7, 43, 48
Debord, Guy 13, 55, 98
deception, cities and 68–71
the *dérive* (drift) 13–14, 98
desire, cities and 88–91
Desire Paths 89–90
Di Buduo, Pino 2, 39, 42, 58, 59, 60, 61, 73, 75, 78, 79, 81, 82
displacement 19, 25, 27, 34
dreams, cities of 32–34
Dublin 18–19, 29

empire, cities and 84–87
Etchells, Tim 27
exercises and workshops: cities of memory 99–106; outdoor-indoor 106–107; stray trips 107–108

Fara in Sabina 35–38; comparison with Rome 42–43; deep past 35–36; Festival Laboratorio Interculturale di Pratiche Teatrali (F.L.I.P.T.) 3, 43, 78, 98, 99, 101, 102; as home for Teatro Potlach 61, 74–75; *Invisible Cities* 39–50, 73, 74, 75, 92–94, 109–129; obscuring or

Index

transforming of architecture 41, 43, 46–47, 49–50; olive trees 36–37; overcoming initial suspicion of Teatro Potlach 72–73; performing itself theatrically 41; performing walking the course of 2019 *Invisible Cities* 110–129; rivers 109; traces of past 35, 36, 37, 42; travelling a part of identity of 74
Fellini, Federico 1, 42, 64, 75
Festival Laboratorio Interculturale di Pratiche Teatrali (F.L.I.P.T.) 3, 43, 78, 98, 99, 101, 102
Five-Second Theatre 28
the *flâneur* 14–15
Forced Entertainment 26–28
Freud, Sigmund 8–9, 62

gift economy approach 78–79
Goodman, Nelson 59
Grotowski, Jerzy 76, 77
Gulyas, Zsofia 47, 92

Harvie, Jen 25

infrastructure, invisible 54–56
intercultural theatre, critique of 79–81
Invisible Cities (Calvino) 2, 20–22, 24, 30, 60, 74, 94–95, 101, 106
Invisible Cities (Teatro Potlach) 2–3, 24, 30, 57–61, 72–83; children dancing 48–49; creating space 92–94; in different locations 42, 73–74; dogs in 44, 48; in Fara in Sabina 39–50, 73, 74, 75, 92–94, 109–129; integrating artisans at work in 47, 59, 79; juxtapositions between theatrical and real 44, 48; Klagenfurt, Austria 73; music 42, 75; obscuring or transforming city architecture 41, 46–47, 49–50, 57–58, 76, 93; performers 42, 43, 44–45, 45–46, 47, 48, 82, 92–93; performing walking the course of 2019 110–129; projections 46, 57, 75, 76, 93; researching cities 58–59, 73–74; residents as participants 42, 79; spectator-travellers 39–40, 43–44, 48, 60–61; stories and backgrounds of festival participants 82; themes for 2019 109–110

Jerusalem 8
Joseph, Rachel 110–129
Joyce, James 18–19, 20
Judaism 7–8

Kaye, Nick 27
Kerouac, Jack 10
Klagenfurt, Austria 73

labour, performances to highlight invisible 28, 47, 59, 79
Lacan, Jacques 9
Laing, Olivia 11–13
Las Vegas 68–71; Circus Circus 69; cultural violence in economy of 69–70, 71; hotel and casino city stage sets 68–69, 70; mass shooting 70–71; the Strip 68–69, 70; theatre scene 70
LGBTQ+ culture, San Francisco 33
'lightness' 78
Linked 25
London 18, 84–87; capital of the world 84–85; capitalism 85; London Museum installation 87; publishing 85–86; theatre 85, 86; Vauxhall Gardens 86–87
London Museum 87
loneliness 11–13
Los Angeles 10

MacCannell, Dean 29
Marx, Karl 8
mass shooting 70–71
Mei Lan Fang 80
memory, cities and 35–38
Mentha, Nathalie 46, 48, 61, 92, 93
Metro journey 55–56
Miller, Graeme 25
modern cities 9–11
monasteries 8
My Point Forward 87
mytho-geography 98

neighbours, visibility of 11–13
New Testament 7
New York City 9–10, 11; apartment dwellers 12–13; hotel stage set 69; travellers to 19
Nights in this City 26–28
novels 19–20; *Invisible Cities* (Calvino) 2, 20–22, 24, 30, 60, 74, 94–95, 101, 106

Odin Teatret 61, 76, 77, 78, 81
olive trees, invisible history of 36–37
Oresteia 4
outdoor-indoor 106–107

panoptic view of city 11
Paris 53–56; bourgeois 14–15; hotel stage set 69; immigrants in 54; invisible infrastructure 54–56; Metro journey 55–56; people-watching 54; tourists 53, 54, 56; tragedy and melodrama 54–55
Pearson, Mike 25, 26
pedestrians, street-level view of city 11

people-watching 54
performing (in) the city 24–31
Pharoah, Anna 28
Plato 6
private behaviours, framed in windows across street 11–13
psychogeography 13–14, 98

Rae, Paul 25, 90
rag-pickers 15–16, 28, 55
Raphael 47, 109, 110
Rear Window 11
Regnoli, Daniela 39–40, 44, 57, 58, 61, 72, 74, 75, 78, 94
religion in cities 6–8
Republic 6
Roman Catholicism 7
Rome 62–67; ancient churches 62; Christian community 7; cinematic otherworlds 64–65; 'Earthly City' of Pagan 6–7; Empire of 65–66; Freud on 8–9, 62; outskirts 65; preserved ruination 66–67; spectacle 66; theatres 66; tourists to 62–64, 66, 67; Vatican 63–64
Rossi, Irene 93

San Francisco 32–34; gentrification 34; LGBTQ+ culture 33; theatrical festivals 33
Sansone, Vincenzo 46, 48, 57, 59, 74, 76
The School of Athens 47, 109
secrets, cities and 53–56
Shakespeare, William 85, 86
Sheffield 26–28
Shklovsky, Viktor 60
Shuji, Terayama 52
Singapore 88–91; *Desire Paths* 88–90; National Day Parade 90; relationship between city and sea 90–91; traces of past and future journeys 88–90
site-specific performance 24, 26–28
Situationists 13–14, 55, 98
Six Memos for the Next Millennium 78
Socrates 6
Solga, Kim 24, 25
solitude 13
Solnit, Rebecca 29, 33
speed, cities and 51–52
Spell#7 88–90
States, Bert 59–60
stray trips 107–108
Surin, Aaron 33

Tambling, Jeremy 18, 19
Taoism 8
Teatro Potlach: *20,000 Leagues Under the Sea* 75; cherry tree 81–82; critique of intercultural approach 81; Festival Laboratorio Interculturale di Pratiche Teatrali (F.L.I.P.T.) 3, 43, 78, 98, 99, 101, 102; gift economy approach 78–79; initial local suspicion of 72–73; juxtapositions between theatrical and real 44, 48; 'lightness' 78; organic growth and sincere relationships 81–82; proximity to Rome 61; roots in Native American potlatch 76, 78; setting up in Fara in Sabina 61, 74–75; 'the third theatre' 76; uncovering memory, culture and identity 59; *see also Invisible Cities* (Teatro Potlach)
theatre: and the city 25; critique of intercultural 79–81; first performance and birth of 96–98; intertwining of city and 52; Las Vegas 70; London 85, 86; Odin Teatret 33, 61, 76, 77, 78, 81; Rome 66; San Francisco 33; space, Italianate 66; transport-based 26–28; *see also Invisible Cities* (Teatro Potlach); Teatro Potlach
theological significance of cities 6–8
thinking (with) the city 4–17
Thompson, Hunter S. 69
Tokyo 51–52
tourism 18–19, 27, 28–29, 41; in Paris 53, 54, 56; in Rome 62–64, 66, 67
transport-based theatre 26–28

Ukeles, Mierle Laderman 28
Ulysses 19

Vatican 7, 63–64, 67
Vauxhall Gardens 86–87
Vauxhall Pleasure 87
Venice 21, 74; hotel stage set 68
violence, cities and 62–67
Vision of Adamnán 7

walking performance, immersive 88–90
Whybrow, Nicolas 25–26
Wilkie, Fiona 27, 28, 87
Woolf, Virginia 18, 85
workshops and exercises: cities of memory 99–106; outdoor-indoor 106–107; stray trips 107–108
World Trade Center 11
Wright & Sites 98
writing the experiences of a city 18–23